RAND

Japan

Domestic Change and Foreign Policy

Mike M. Mochizuki

Prepared for the
Office of the Secretary of Defense

National Defense
Research Institute

The following report was produced under the aegis of a project entitled *Reevaluating Asia: Regional Indicators and U.S. Policy*, which
represents a multiyear effort to analyze the political-military, social,
and economic dimensions of change in the Asia-Pacific region over
the next 10–15 years. The goal of the project is to delineate a set of
indicators within the various dimensions. An indicator is an event,
process, or development that portends possible changes with negative implications for core U.S. policy assumptions and regional security objectives.

This document should be of interest to regional specialists, those in
the Department of Defense, and others seeking information about
the relationship between the United States and Japan. Other reports
in the project for *Reevaluating Asia: Regional Indicators and U.S.
Policy* cover the following topics:

- Asia's Changing Security Environment: Sources of Adversity for
  U.S. Policy

- Change in Taiwan and Potential Adversity in the Strait

- China: Domestic Change and Foreign Policy.

This research was conducted for the Under Secretary of Defense for
Policy within the International Security and Defense Policy Center in
RAND's National Defense Research Institute (NDRI). NDRI is a fed-
erally funded research and development center sponsored by the
Office of the Secretary of Defense, the Joint Staff, and the defense
agencies. Supplemental funding was also provided by the RAND
Center for Asia-Pacific Policy.

CONTENTS

Preface iii

Figures ix

Tables xi

Summary of Key Findings xiii

Acknowledgments xv

Acronyms xvii

Chapter One
    INTRODUCTION 1

Chapter Two
    POLITICAL REALIGNMENT 3
    Causes of Political Realignment 5
        Changes in the International System 5
        Split in Ruling Liberal Democratic Party 6
        Public Discontent Regarding Corruption 7
        Formation of a Non-LDP Coalition Government 8
    Key Political Trends 11
        Decline of Traditional Ideological Rifts and Increase in
            Fluid Party Alignments 11
        Weakening of Political Cohesion Within Parties 13
        Political Maneuvering in Response to the New
            Electoral System 15
        Increase in Bureaucratic Power During Period of
            Political Fluidity 19

Future Scenarios   21
    Competition Among Three Political Forces   22
    Loose Two-Party System   22
    Fragmented Multiparty System   23

Chapter Three
ECONOMIC TRANSFORMATION   25
Causes of the Economic Recession   26
    Collapse of the Bubble Economy   26
    Excessive Productive Capacity   26
    Yen Appreciation   27
Debate About Economic Policy   28
    Expansionary Fiscal Policy   30
    Changes in Tax Policy   31
    Economic Deregulation   33
Effect on Industrial Structure and the Labor Market   35
    Changes in *Keiretsu* and Subcontracting
        Relationships   35
    Labor Market Fluidity   36
    Increase in Foreign Workers   38
Implications for Foreign Trade and Investments   39
    Deepening of Japan's Economic Linkages with East
        Asia   39
    Weakening of U.S. Economic Leverage in the Region ..   45

Chapter Four
ATTITUDINAL CHANGE   47
Elite and Intellectual Opinion   47
    Sharpened Debate Among Mainstream Security Policy
        Analysts: Great Power Internationalism Versus
        Civilian Internationalism   47
    Growing Critiques of Japan's Past Approach to
        Economic Development   51
    Rise of "New Asianism"   54
Public Opinion   56
    Generally Positive Views of the United States   56
    Less Positive Views Toward Ties with Other Asian
        Countries as Alternatives to the U.S. Relationship ...   61
    Continuity in Security Policy Coupled with
        Constitutional Reform   62
Generational Change   65

Chapter Five
   IMPLICATIONS FOR JAPANESE FOREIGN POLICY AND
      EXTERNAL BEHAVIOR   69
   Basic Parameters of Japanese Foreign Policy and External
      Behavior   69
   Political-Military Dimension   70
      Review of the National Defense Program Outline   70
      North Korean Nuclear Issue   77
      Possible Emergence of Great Power Nationalism   80
   Foreign Economic Dimension   82
      Economic Relations with the United States   82
      Asia-Pacific Regionalism and Economic Integration
         with East Asia   85

Chapter Six
   CONCLUSIONS   89

Bibliography   95

FIGURES

3.1. Japan's Annual Real GDP Growth Rate 25
3.2. Japan's Foreign Direct Investments 40
3.3. Japan's Two-Way Trade with the United States and
     East Asia 41
3.4. Japan's Exports to the United States, East Asia, and
     Western Europe 42
3.5. Japan's Trade Balance with East Asia and the United
     States 42
3.6. U.S. Trade Balance with East Asia and Japan 43
4.1. Japanese Public Opinion: Feeling of Affinity Toward
     the United States, China, South Korea, and Russia . . . 57
4.2. Japanese Views of America and American Views of
     Japan 58
4.3. Japanese Public Opinion: State of U.S.-Japan
     Relations (*Yomiuri Shimbun* Survey) 58
4.4. Japanese Public Opinion: State of U.S.-Japan
     Relations (Prime Minister's Office Survey) 59
4.5. Japanese Views of America, China, and South Korea . . 61
4.6. Japanese Public Opinion: Protecting Japan's
     Security 63
4.7. Japanese Public Opinion: Size of the Defense
     Budget 64
4.8. Public Attitude Toward Constitutional Revision 64

4.1. Japanese Public Opinion: Country That Is Most Threatening 59

4.2. Japanese Public Opinion: U.S.-Japan Economic Relations.................................. 60

4.3. Japanese Public Opinion: Issue of Constitutional Revision 65

SUMMARY OF KEY FINDINGS

This report analyzes the implications of political, economic, and attitudinal developments within Japan for the evolution of Japanese foreign policy over the next 10 to 15 years, especially policy toward the Asia-Pacific region. The purpose of such analysis is to discern whether and in what manner the changes that have taken place within Japan since the early 1990s could prove adverse to U.S. interests in Asia. This analysis treats Japanese domestic political, economic, and public opinion trends as largely independent variables. Also, important external influences upon Japanese policy—for example, the actions of critical actors such as the United States—are discussed primarily within the context of such domestic factors.

This report concludes the following:

- The end of one-party dominance in Japan is likely to produce a prolonged period of political fluidity and weak governments, thereby impeding timely decisions for dealing with the changing international environment and strengthening the power of national bureaucrats.

- Notwithstanding this political fluidity, Japanese foreign policy is likely to fall within the following parameters: (1) maintenance of the security relationship with the United States in some form; (2) promotion of multilateral security fora in the Asia-Pacific region as a complement to the U.S.-Japan security relationship; (3) increasing Japanese participation in the United Nations in the security as well as other realms; and (4) closer integration with other East Asian economies through trade, investments, and technology transfers and support for the process of Asia-Pacific Economic Cooperation (APEC).

• While initially reinforcing moderation in the security policy debate, the political realignment process could also lay the foundations for repolarization by permitting the rise of a stridently nationalistic force, especially in the context of deteriorating economic relations with the United States. Political realignment in Japan could also lead to a weakening of the U.S. security commitment to Japan, increasing Chinese geopolitical assertiveness, and to the emergence of a hostile, reunified Korea.

• Structural recession is causing Japanese leaders to reexamine the efficacy of economic policies and business practices that have served Japan so well for nearly four decades. Also, market forces are causing Japanese firms to reduce their productive capacities and gradually to move toward more flexible employment and subcontracting practices.

• By "exporting" export-led development to other East Asian countries, Japan poses a trade challenge to the United States both directly (from Japanese exports) and indirectly (from non-Japanese East Asian exports); and the United States is likely to remain the primary absorber of both Japanese and East Asian exports despite the large increase in Japanese trade with the rest of East Asia.

• Japan will become less accommodating to U.S. pressures on trade issues as its center of economic gravity shifts to East Asia and will increasingly turn to multilateral institutions and settings to resist American unilateralism.

• Although the Japanese public is unlikely to view the countries of East Asia as attractive strategic alternatives to the United States and other Western states for international alignments, support will grow on behalf of Japan playing a bridging role between East Asia on the one hand and the United States and the West on the other.

ACKNOWLEDGMENTS

Numerous individuals assisted me in preparing this report. Yoshinobu Konomi, Asahiko Mihara, Satoshi Morimoto, Matashiro Nakagawa, Masaomi Omae, and Kin-ichi Yoshihara kindly arranged many interviews with Japanese politicians, bureaucratic officials, journalists, business leaders, and scholars. Kenneth Pyle of the University of Washington provided excellent comments and criticisms on an earlier draft of this report. My former colleagues at RAND—Julia Lowell, Courtney Purrington, Michael Swaine, and Rachel Swanger—also gave me perceptive critiques. Although I was unable to incorporate all of their suggestions, this report is a better document because of their input. I would also like to thank Deborah Elms and Jessica Steele for preparing the tables and figures.

ACRONYMS

ACSA	Acquisition and Cross-Servicing Agreement
APEC	Asia-Pacific Economic Cooperation
ASEAN	Association of Southeast Asian Nations
DIDG	Defense Issues Discussion Group
DSP	Democratic Socialist Party
EAEC	East Asian Economic Caucus
FDI	Foreign Direct Investments
FILP	Fiscal Investment and Loan Program
GATT	General Agreement on Tariffs and Trade
GDP	Gross Domestic Product
JDA	Japan Defense Agency
JNP	Japan New Party
LDP	Liberal Democratic Party
MITI	Ministry of International Trade and Industry
MOF	Ministry of Finance
MOFA	Ministry of Foreign Affairs
NAFTA	North American Free Trade Agreement
NATO	North Atlantic Treaty Organization
NDPO	National Defense Program Outline
NGO	Nongovernmental Organization
ODA	Official Development Assistance
PKF	Peacekeeping Forces
PKO	Peacekeeping Operation
PMO	Prime Minister's Office
PPP	Purchasing Power Parity
SDF	Self-Defense Forces
SDPJ	Social Democratic Party of Japan

TMD	Theater Missile Defense
U.N.	United Nations
WTO	World Trade Organization

Chapter One

INTRODUCTION

Japan is at an historic crossroads. The end of the Cold War has removed the structural underpinnings of the international system from which Japan has benefited enormously. No other major power gained as much in both economic and security terms as Japan did by aligning with the United States in the Soviet-American competition. But with the geopolitical glue that held the U.S.-Japan relationship together gone, Japan is increasingly anxious not only about its relations with the United States, but also about the appropriate role for the country in world affairs.

The choices that Japanese leaders make during the next five or so years will determine Japan's international outlook well into the 21st century. This current period is in many ways analogous to the historical era of 1947–1955, when Japan's security and economic policy directions were charted and the institutional foundations for these policies were laid. Most of what came after was not much more than a logical working out of these basic policies in the context of marginal changes in the international environment. Similarly, what happens in Japan in the next five years and how Japan interacts with its external environment will define the overall parameters of its foreign policy for the post–Cold War world. Three domestic processes will play a critical role in determining Japan's strategic choices during this age of international uncertainty: political realignment, structural economic transformation, and change in elite and public opinion.

The process of political realignment will define the kind of party system that will eventually emerge after the end of nearly 40 years of

Liberal Democratic Party dominance. It will affect the degree to which electoral and parliamentary politics, as opposed to bureaucratic power, will shape the foreign policy agenda and concrete policy outcomes. At this point, the realignment process appears to support a general depolarization of the security policy debate. As a result, Japanese voters will be able to voice their preferences between two mainstream, realistic alternatives. But at the same time, a nationalistic political force could emerge and contest elections by openly criticizing Japan's close relations with the United States.

The process of economic transformation triggered by yen appreciation and a deep structural recession presents the possibility that the Japanese economy will become more receptive to foreign goods and services and be driven more by domestic demand than by foreign economic expansion. This would go far in reestablishing a stable equilibrium in U.S.-Japan relations. But the current economic challenges could also reinforce Japan's neomercantilistic policies and behavior. Such an outcome would not only exacerbate economic tensions between Japan and the United States, but also provoke a bitter competitive struggle for East Asian markets.

Changes in elite opinion have redefined the domestic debate regarding Japan's role in international affairs. The salient debate is now about the appropriate modalities of international cooperation, rather than about the wisdom of such cooperation itself. Regarding economic policy, opinion leaders are beginning to question Japan's adherence to what might be called "developmental corporatism." But proponents of both liberal and social democratic reforms confront formidable political and institutional obstacles. A consensus among opinion leaders has emerged that Japan should devote more attention to the East Asian dimension of its foreign policy, but the debate has only begun about the concrete policy implications of this "re-Asianization." Mass opinion exhibits much more continuity than elite opinion. Nevertheless, there are clear signs of increasing public anxiety about the state of U.S.-Japan relations. Japanese citizens are also becoming more receptive to considering constitutional revision.

This report will examine in some detail each of these three sets of domestic trends. It will close by analyzing the implications of these internal developments for Japan's foreign policies and external behavior.

Chapter Two

POLITICAL REALIGNMENT

During the Cold War era, the Liberal Democratic Party (LDP) provided a robust political foundation for Japan's security linkage with the United States. The party's fall from power in August 1993 followed by the advent of coalition governments, however, is unlikely to change this foreign policy orientation in the near future. Although the seven-party coalition that succeeded the LDP encompassed the heretofore neutralist Social Democratic Party of Japan (SDPJ), the coalition partners agreed to continue the LDP's basic policies. Indeed, the shift in the SDPJ's stance from unarmed neutralism toward support for maintaining the U.S.-Japan Security Treaty made possible in June 1994 the emergence of an LDP-SDPJ coalition (along with the Shinto Sakigake—New Party Harbinger—or the "small reformist party") and the election of Japan's first social democratic premier since 1948. But one should not overstate the case for continuity. The process of political realignment could affect the general political context of Japanese security policy in several ways—some positively, others negatively.

First, the events of 1993 brought to an end the so-called "1955-system" in which interparty competition (and even collusion) was largely shaped by the Liberal Democratic and Socialist parties. Consequently, the sharp ideological division that had defined the context of security policymaking during the Cold War era has given way to a more moderate debate among centrist alternatives. Political support for the extreme alternatives of the nationalist right or the neutralist left has waned. To the extent that security policy becomes an issue in this period of political transition, the salient debate is likely to be within the parameters of an alliance with the United States.

Second, political realignment could sharpen the *public* debate about concrete security policy questions. During the last two decades, the public discussion of security issues diverged from the debate within the elite foreign policy community. Whereas the public discussion focused on the alternatives of a pro-American realism and an idealistic pacifism, the elite debate with real policy consequences centered around questions of alliance burden-sharing, the relative weight of military and nonmilitary means to enhance security, and constitutional interpretation. As the interparty policy positions become less polarized in the course of realignment, the public discourse on security issues will become more linked to the concrete policy choices confronting government officials.

Third, although the realignment process could initially reinforce moderation in the security policy debate, it could also lay the foundations for repolarization. Under conservative one-party rule, the Liberal Democrats effectively subsumed conservative nationalism, and the ultranationalist right was relegated either to the seamy world of the criminal underground or to the political fringe. To the extent that these elements were interested in foreign policy, they directed their animosity toward the communist states of the Soviet Union and China. In the current context, further fragmentation of the conservative forces could yield a stridently nationalistic force that would compete for support in the mainstream of electoral politics. And with the decline of communism and chronic frictions in U.S.-Japan economic relations, such a force could direct its hostility toward the United States.

Fourth, even without this repolarization of politics, the end of one-party dominance could produce a prolonged period of political fluidity and weak governments. Japan would then have great difficulty making decisive and hard choices to deal effectively with the changing international environment. Under these circumstances, Japanese citizens may increasingly feel that their country is being buffeted by hostile external forces. Voices for a more assertive and independent foreign policy backed by a stronger military could become more powerful. At the same time, political instability will enhance the national bureaucracy's role in developing long-term diplomatic and security policy. But this bureaucratically formulated policy may lack the political support necessary for effective implementation.

The first step in this process of political reform was the adoption of a new electoral system involving a hybrid of single-seat constituencies and proportional representation to replace the old system of multi-seat medium-sized districts. A complex interaction of several factors will shape the dynamics of further political realignment: personal relationships among politicians, the organizational capabilities of specific leaders and their allies, the electoral calculations and prospects of individual politicians under the new electoral system, and differences on policy positions among politicians. Eventually, this complicated process of fragmentation, realignment, and reaggregation could yield political rifts based more on policy differences among politicians than on patron-client relations.

CAUSES OF POLITICAL REALIGNMENT

Several interrelated developments triggered the realignment process that began in the summer of 1993:

- Changes in the international system
- Split in the ruling Liberal Democratic Party
- Public discontent about political corruption
- Formation of a non-LDP coalition government.

Changes in the International System

The underlying cause of political realignment was the end of the Cold War. To a large extent, it was the Cold War that brought about the 1955-system in which political conflict and even collusion were defined by the Liberal Democratic and the Japan Socialist parties. Consequently, the end of the Cold War made the demise of the 1955-system possible. First of all, the collapse of the Soviet Union and with it the end of the bipolar international system reduced the saliency of the ideological conflict between conservatives and progressives on security policy. Second, the failure of communism and even socialism undermined the appeal and credibility of the traditional left in Japan. In the 1950s, the challenge of leftist ascendancy galvanized the conservatives to amalgamate and establish a one-party dominant system. In turn, the decline of the left weakened this centripetal force within the LDP. Consequently, political alliances between ruling and opposition party groups became more possible. Finally, the emergence of new international challenges aroused a number of key political elites to transform the political system so that Japan might be better able to respond to these external challenges. The Persian Gulf crisis of 1990–1991 steered the LDP to forge a coalition with the Komeito (Clean Government Party) and the Democratic Socialist Party (DSP) on Japanese participation in U.N. peacekeeping operations as well as Japanese financial contributions to Operations Desert Shield and Storm. Both developments weakened the political position of the two traditional leftist parties: the SDPJ and the Japan Communist Party.

Although international change established the basis for a redrawing of Japan's political map, internal issues such as political corruption and political coalition strategies have shaped the concrete character of realignment.

Split in Ruling Liberal Democratic Party

The Keiseikai or Takeshita faction, the largest and dominant faction in the LDP, split as a result of a power struggle. This intrafactional struggle was provoked by the resignation of Shin Kanemaru as Keiseikai chairman, LDP vice president, and later National Diet member in the wake of a tax evasion scandal. After being defeated in this power play, Ichiro Ozawa formed his own faction under the banner of Reform 21, began to argue vigorously for structural changes in Japanese politics, and started to explore possible alliances with some of the opposition parties. Ozawa's ultimate objective now is to break the traditional pattern of Japanese politics that has involved intricate factional balancing for official positions, an emphasis on political brokering to serve local constituencies, and the obfuscation of public debates on important policy questions. The irony of Ozawa as a reformer is that he developed his political skills and influence by being at the heart of the old LDP power structure and its largest faction. Early in his political career, Ozawa was taken under the wing of Kakuei Tanaka, the master of distributive politics and patronage. As Tanaka's power faded, he then became the protégé of Shin Kanemaru—another wielder of power through patronage. Ozawa's embrace of political reform did not come because he wanted to rid Japan of money politics and corruption in response to public outcries. Rather he saw an urgent need to transform the political system so that Japan could respond more effectively to the changing external environment. As LDP secretary general during the Iraq-Kuwait crisis, Ozawa saw how the inability of Japan to deal more effectively with the crisis jeopardized Japan's national honor and risked international isolation. He would like to see the emergence of a two-party system; a strengthening of executive power; Japan's development into a "normal" country, that is, one that can freely deploy military forces abroad for the purpose of collective defense as well as self-defense; and eventually a revision of the postwar constitution. For him, changing the electoral system so that the bulk of the National Diet members in the lower house would run in single-member districts is the best way to achieve these objectives (Ryuzaki, 1993; Watanabe, 1992; Itagaki, 1993). Immediately after the passage of the no-confidence resolution against Prime Minister Miyazawa in July 1993, Ozawa and his associates formed the party Shinseito (awkwardly translated into English as Rebirth Party).

Public Discontent Regarding Corruption

Widespread public discontent about successive instances of political corruption contributed to the realignment process. This was reflected by a sharp drop in popular support for the LDP in numerous public opinion polls. When Prime Minister Kiichi Miyazawa failed to enact political reform legislation, Ozawa joined forces with opposition parties to pass a no-confidence motion against Miyazawa in the National Diet. Although the LDP managed to maintain its preelection parliamentary strength, it failed to garner a single-party majority in the July 1993 general election. More important, however, was the dramatic rise of various new parties, with roots in the LDP, that capitalized on the popular dissatisfaction with the existing political order. The most striking was the Nihon Shinto (Japan New Party or JNP) led by former LDP National Diet member and prefectural governor, Morihiro Hosokawa, who created the party in May 1992. In the July 1992 House of Councilors election, the JNP won 8 percent of the vote and four seats on a platform that stressed political reform, an end to political corruption and money politics, administrative decentralization, and policies that favor average Japanese who "make a living" (*seikatsu-sha*). The party itself encompassed three subgroups. One involved the people with whom Hosokawa had developed a personal working relationship on behalf of reform. Another consisted of the young political activists trained in the Matsushita Seikei Juku (the Matsushita Political Economic Institute). The Matsushita institute was established by the legendary founder of the Matsushita electronics conglomerate, Konosuke Matsushita, to develop young Japanese leaders who were not wedded to traditional business and political practices. Finally, there were the political outsiders who have had little or no previous contact with Hosokawa, but who came forth to run under the JNP reform banner in the July 1993 House of Representatives election and won.

The other new reformist party with LDP roots to emerge was the Shinto Sakigake led by Masayoshi Takemura. The Sakigake consists primarily of relatively young LDP politicians who had worked actively for political reform within the ruling party. After recognizing that real reform was impossible without an end to the 1955-system, this group decided as early as the spring of 1993 to bolt the LDP. Unlike most of the JNP parliamentarians, the 13 Sakigake members in the lower house have had experience running for office and getting reelected. Their electoral base tends to be much more organized and stable along the lines of traditional *koenkai* (support organizations).

Formation of a Non-LDP Coalition Government

The fourth causal factor of political realignment was the formation of a seven-party coalition government consisting of all of the former opposition parties (except the Communist Party) as well as the new parties and excluding the LDP. After losing its parliamentary majority in the July 1993 elections, the LDP could still have remained in power by pulling the new parties into an LDP-led coalition. But Ozawa and his Shinseito outmaneuvered the Liberal Democrats. He enticed both Hosokawa of the JNP and Takemura of the Sakigake away from forming a coalition with the LDP by supporting the two of them for the positions of prime minister and chief cabinet secretary, respectively. At the same time, he worked closely with the Komeito, the Democratic Socialist Party, and the Social Democratic League to negotiate a revolutionary interparty agreement regarding basic policy—especially in the area of foreign affairs. By accepting this agreement, the SDPJ recognized its political weakness and began its decisive shift away from its policy of unarmed neutrality. After an electoral surge in the 1989 upper house and the 1990 lower house elections under Takako Doi's leadership, the party failed to consolidate its popular support by adopting more imaginative and realistic policies and by expanding its organizational base beyond labor unions. The irony of the July 1993 election was that after suffering its worst defeat at the polls, the SDPJ became a government party for the first time since 1948.

The wide range of policy views among the seven coalition parties made the task of governing particularly difficult. The one thing that kept the coalition together was a commitment to reforming national politics, especially the electoral system. But as soon as the political reform bills neared National Diet passage, deep rifts in the coalition appeared (Asahi Shimbun Seijibu, 1994). The first was the falling out between Hosokawa and Takemura. Originally, the JNP and the Sakigake were slated to merge, but differences about political strategy and policy broke up the Hosokawa-Takemura partnership. Hosokawa became much more supportive of Ozawa's agenda of pushing toward a two-party system and of approving a consumption tax hike. Hosokawa's shift toward Ozawa steered Takemura to cultivate closer ties with former LDP colleagues—especially those most supportive of political reform, as well as SDPJ leaders. The Ozawa-Takemura conflict went beyond personal rivalry to substantive policy differences (Itagaki, 1994). In contrast to Ozawa's goal of a two-party system with strong executive power, Takemura favored a moderate multiparty system and coalition governments. The contrast was stronger in terms of foreign policy. Ozawa saw Japanese participation in U.N. peacekeeping operations as a first step toward Japan becoming a "normal" country. Takemura's aim, however, was to strengthen the peacekeeping activities of the United Nations, but not to expand the Self-Defense Forces (Japan's military) beyond the mission of homeland defense in a strict sense. Whereas Ozawa wanted Japan to become an active player in the international security arena (including a permanent seat on the U.N. Security Council),

Takemura sought to soft-pedal Japan's political-military role in international affairs and to stress nonmilitary means for promoting global stability. He was reluctant about pushing Japan's case for permanent membership in the U.N. Security Council and the issue of constitutional revision. In short, he wanted to keep Japan "a small country " (Takemura, 1994, pp. 173–212; Tanaka, 1994, pp. 161–163). He is also more eager than Ozawa to press for administrative decentralization and policies favorable to consumers.

In addition to the Ozawa-Takemura rivalry, the SDPJ found it increasingly difficult to work with Ozawa's Shinseito. The rice liberalization issue in December 1993 in the context of the General Agreement on Tariffs and Trade (GATT) Uruguay Round negotiations forced the SDPJ to abandon its strict protectionist policy on rice and weakened the party's political cohesion. Then, Ozawa, in cooperation with the Finance Ministry, pressed the Hosokawa Cabinet to link an income tax cut with a consumption tax hike. This move was especially hard to swallow given the SDPJ's long-term opposition to the consumption tax. The party also suspected that Ozawa had the ulterior political motive of wanting to engineer an SDPJ split as part of his grand design to remake Japanese politics. This intention became clearer in the wake of Prime Minister Hosokawa's resignation when Ozawa supported the formation of a parliamentary group known as the Kaishin (Innovation) consisting of the Shinseito, the Komeito, the DSP, and JNP. In response to the Kaishin, the Sakigake, the SDPJ, and a few defectors from the Nihon Shinto formed an informal group of their own: Seiun (Blue Cloud).[1]

The defection of the SDPJ and Sakigake from the seven-party coalition forced the remaining coalition partners to form a short-lived minority government around Tsutomu Hata, the nominal leader of the Shinseito. In the meantime, Takemura of the Sakigake worked closely with SDPJ chairman Tomiichi Murayama and LDP leaders Yohei Kono and Yoshiro Mori to lay the groundwork for a three-party majoritarian coalition. Last minute maneuvers by Ozawa's allies to bring the SDPJ back into the original coalition failed. This was not at all surprising since Ozawa himself was interested in causing not only

[1]For a detailed journal narrative of these developments, see Asahi Shimbun Seijibu, 1994.

another large split in the LDP, but also a breakup of the SDPJ itself. Immediately after the passage of the national budget in June 1994, an LDP-Sakigake-SDPJ alliance forced Prime Minister Hata to resign and then ascended to power by supporting Murayama for the prime ministership.

About six months later, the former coalition parties that were now out of power coalesced to form the Shinshinto (the New Frontier Party). Although the alliance between Ichiro Ozawa of the Shinseito and Yuichi Ichikawa of the Komeito was the core of this new party, neither leader could take the helm because of their political liabilities. Ozawa's intimate links to the traditional LDP pattern of client-centered politics and corruption along with his high-handed political tactics made him vulnerable to media and public attacks if he assumed the top post in the Shinshinto. Ichikawa's association with the Komeito and its religious patron organization, Sokagakkai, would make it difficult to broaden the appeal of the new party if he took the lead. Consequently, the Shinshinto turned to former prime minister Toshiki Kaifu who had been a popular prime minister despite his ineffectiveness. He had the advantage of presenting a clean image to the public while being easily manipulated by the real powerbrokers.

KEY POLITICAL TRENDS

During this period of political fluidity, four general trends are likely to shape Japan's political landscape over the next five years:

- Decline of traditional ideological rifts and increase in third party alignments
- Weakening of political cohesion within parties
- Political maneuvering in response to the new electoral system
- Increase in bureaucratic power during a period of political fluidity.

Decline of Traditional Ideological Rifts and Increase in Fluid Party Alignments

The formation of a coalition between the LDP and SDPJ vividly illustrates how the old Cold War era rifts that had defined party competition have dissipated. In participating in governing coalitions, the Social Democrats have been forced to abandon their previous idealistic policies and to face up to governmental responsibility. The SDPJ has now shifted its policies in directions that were unimaginable only a few years ago. Not only has it come out in support of the security treaty with the United States, it has openly recognized the constitutionality of the Self-Defense Forces (SDF). It has even begun to accept SDF participation in U.N. peacekeeping operations. This SDPJ convergence with the political mainstream on security policy now makes possible innumerable coalition alternatives based upon opportunistic political calculations, rather than on commitments to policy positions.

This, however, does not mean that policies will not matter at all in political alignments. One can identify substantive differences about a variety of policy issues. On security policy, there are those like Ozawa who would like to transform Japan into a normal country by embracing the notion of "collective self-defense," by pushing for a permanent seat on the U.N. Security Council, and by raising the issue of constitutional revision. There are others like Takemura of the Sakigake and Kono of the LDP who prefer that Japan contribute to international security primarily through nonmilitary means as a "civilian power." Regarding economic policy, some politicians favor making greater progress on administrative reform and decentralization first before raising the consumption tax, while others see the urgency of linking a consumption tax hike to the current income tax cut. Although these are not major ideological differences, they do have concrete implications for policy.

What complicates political alignments now is that the various policy tendencies cut across formal party organizations. For example, LDP politicians who support constitutional revision and a stronger defense force probably have more in common with members of the Shinseito than their more dovish LDP colleagues. But many in the LDP right wing are adamant about not cooperating with the Shinseito because of their personal animosity toward Ozawa. The right wing of the SDPJ probably identifies more with members of the DSP on a variety of economic and social policy questions than with the left wing of their own party. The policy differences between the Sakigake and DSP are hard to fathom; yet, they are now on opposite political sides. All of this has had the effect of confusing the public about the policy implications of various coalitions.

Weakening of Political Cohesion Within Parties

As political alignments have become more fluid, cohesion within political parties themselves has also weakened. In the case of the LDP, this has involved episodic defections. First, there was the departure of Hosokawa from the LDP fold to form the JNP in 1992. Then came the departure of Takemura's group and Ozawa's Reform 21 faction in July 1993. Further hemorrhaging took place in the context of electoral reform, the process to select Hosokawa's successor, and the formation of the LDP-SDPJ-Sakigake coalition. But the LDP has so far avoided another major split comparable to the July 1993 defections. Indeed the primary preoccupation of LDP leadership (President Yohei Kono and Secretary General Yoshiro Mori) has been the maintenance of party unity. There were some signs that Michio Watanabe might join forces with Ozawa as a way to secure the prime ministership after Hosokawa's resignation. He had lost to Kono during the party presidential election held after Miyazawa's resignation. Long noted for his hawkish views, Watanabe does share Ozawa's desire to remake Japan into a more normal country (Watanabe et al., 1994). But his faction strongly resisted for two reasons: concerns about Ozawa's ties with Sokagakkai and deep personal animosity toward Ozawa. Even those in the LDP who support Ozawa's vision of a more assertive Japan remain angry about his treacherous and arrogant behavior. This widespread anger toward and distrust of Ozawa personally have helped to keep the LDP together.

While the party itself has avoided a large-scale defection, the LDP's factional system has weakened considerably. While the LDP was out of power from August 1993 through June 1994, the factional bosses lost one of the critical levers of power: their ability to promote candidates from their own factions for cabinet and top party posts. Even after returning to power in July 1994, because the LDP had to share cabinet ministerships with the SDPJ and Sakigake, the appointment powers of factional bosses have not revived to the degree that was the case during the heyday of LDP dominance. Moreover, factional bosses no longer serve as the major conduits of political funds to politicians. In many cases now, the factional members themselves pay dues to the faction to sustain the group (LDP National Diet member, 1993). Notwithstanding the cases of intense interfactional conflict during the period of LDP dominance, the factional system did help to maintain party cohesion through a cartelized pattern of conflict management. The factions worked to connect the party leadership and the rank and file and avoid the frontbench-back-bench splits that have created problems for many European political parties. As the factions decline as aggregators of political interests, rank-and-file revolts are likely to become more common. This may open up opportunities for ambitious younger leaders to mobilize on behalf of party revitalization. The danger, of course, is that it also makes further party defections more probable.

Unlike the LDP, defections from the SDPJ have been more limited. There has, however, been notable backbench discontent. This discontent erupted during the following occasions: (1) liberalization of the rice market in the context of the GATT Uruguay Round trade negotiations in December 1993, (2) National Diet vote on legislation to change the electoral system, and (3) the decision to join the LDP and Sakigake in a coalition government. Thus far, the party has continued to stay together simply as a matter of survival. Their primary source of influence comes from having some 70 lower house seats. Further defections would therefore dramatically diminish their attractiveness as a coalition partner. Despite sharp interparty differences about coalition policy, there appears to be a general party consensus in favor of government participation as the most attractive path to party revitalization. The shift in security policy has not triggered an open party split because it was Murayama, a member of the party left wing, and not a right-wing leader who engineered this change. Nevertheless, the SDPJ still carries within itself sharp differences in policy and ideology that could erupt into a major split. Staying in power may therefore be the best way to reduce the risk of this happening.

Political cohesion is problematic in the Shinshinto as well. Even before the Shinshinto's inauguration in December 1994, the new party's constituent parties had been experiencing internal turmoil. The Democratic Socialist Party experienced a sharp conflict between its top two leaders about coalition policy. The Japan New Party began to disintegrate quickly after Hosokawa's fall from power. Even the

Shinseito experienced intraparty tensions after the recent tactical failures of Ozawa to split the LDP and the SDPJ. After the amalgamation of these various groups to form the Shinshinto, intraparty cohesion and management has become even more problematic. Key members of the Shinseito who had bolted the LDP because they wanted to transform politics are now dissatisfied that the merger has diluted the reformist impulse of the Shinseito.

Political Maneuvering in Response to the New Electoral System

In January 1994, the National Diet passed a package of four bills changing the electoral system and tightening the regulations on political fund-raising. The new electoral system for the House of Representatives will consist of 300 single-seat districts and 11 electoral regions that will elect a total of 200 representatives on a proportional representation basis. To correct the malapportionment between urban and rural districts, the reform legislation also mandated keeping the vote-weight discrepancy across districts to a minimum of 1:2. This change could theoretically increase the political influence of urban consumers and salaried workers relative to the protectionist farmers.

Reformers argued that the objectives of changing the electoral system and preventing political corruption by revising the system of political funding were inextricably linked. The system of medium-sized electoral districts encouraged corruption because large parties like the Liberal Democratic Party had to field more than one candidate per district. Therefore, politicians mobilized voters not by making policy appeals, but by distributing selective benefits to constituents and maintaining costly support organizations. A shift to single-member districts (as proposed by the coalition government) would encourage both party amalgamation and electoral competition based on public policy debates. There were opponents of this type of electoral reform in both the LDP and the SDPJ. Many Social Democrats believed that the adoption of single-member districts would cause the SDPJ to lose so many seats that it would cease to be a major party if it survived at all. Some Liberal Democrats opposed electoral reform because the subsequent redistricting could drastically alter their old constituencies, placing them at an electoral disadvantage. Others argued that single-member districts would increase the power of party leaderships over the rank and file and discourage political entrepreneurship (Sato, Seizaburo, 1993).

Now that the redistricting plan under the new electoral system has been implemented, incumbent politicians are likely to make their own individual calculations about what party affiliation will best serve their electoral interests. This could prompt further party defections and shifts in political alignments. The new system will encourage amalgamation of the various political forces into two to three major groupings. A mix of policy differences, personal relationships, and organizational linkages will determine the lines of political rift. The passage of electoral reform will release the centrifugal forces on basic policy questions and is likely to result in new alignments that cut across the government-opposition divide. The outcome of the elections will hinge not only on voter preferences, but also on the ability of the various parties to cooperate by fielding joint candidates or even by merging. Assuming a continuity of voter preferences and no cooperation among the existing parties, the new electoral system will work to the LDP's advantage. Various estimates predict that under such circumstances, the LDP would win a single-party majority of 285 seats out of 500. If the current three-party governing coalition of the LDP, SDPJ, and the Sakigake can cooperate as a single electoral group, then this alliance could win as many as 357 seats (based upon the electoral performance of the individual parties in the last election) (*Yomiuri Shimbun*, August 12, 1994). But neither is likely to happen. The non-LDP parties will have strong incentives to cooperate, and competitive pressures and policy differences will prevent the LDP and SDPJ from forming a tight electoral alliance.

A key determinant of electoral politics under the new system will be the Shinshinto's ability to sustain its unity and field a strong slate of candidates in all 300 single-member districts of the lower house. Most of the original Shinseito lower house representatives have relatively secure support bases that are likely to survive under the new electoral system. The mass mobilization power of the Sokagakkai, the religious organization with which the Komeito is affiliated, will also strengthen the electoral prospects of Shinshinto. Journal reports suggest that the Sokagakkai funneled large amounts of money into Shinseito coffers during the July 1993 general election (Goto, 1994).

Under the new electoral system, the Sokagakkai could mobilize its mammoth membership (estimated at about 8–10 million) on behalf of candidates endorsed by the Shinshinto. What makes this a potentially critical factor in the evolution of party politics is the iron loyalty of Sokagakkai members during election campaigns. Even though floating voters are increasingly important in determining electoral outcomes, a candidate backed by the Sokagakkai will certainly have a competitive edge. Moreover, the Sokagakkai with its large membership, tax breaks accorded to religious bodies, and massive publication campaigns is one of the wealthiest nonbusiness organizations in Japan. The support of Sokagakkai, however, is likely to present a dilemma for the Shinshinto. While Sokagakkai's support will enhance the Shinshinto's electoral capabilities, it could also cause other political partners to turn away because of apprehensions about the role of militant religious groups in politics.

The single-district system is also posing dilemmas for the LDP. In a number of districts, conflicts have emerged among veteran politicians about who will get the official party endorsement. Moreover, maximizing the number of LDP candidates may crowd out viable candidacies among its government coalition partners, the SDPJ and the Sakigake. Some of these difficulties can be resolved by routing the more problematic cases to the proportional representational constituencies. But several leading political figures have resisted this maneuver out of concerns that running from the propositional representation (PR) constituencies constitutes second-class status.

The situation is most serious for the SDPJ. Given the party's declining popularity and the loss of its raison d'être, Social Democratic politicians fear political extinction under the new electoral system. Many now realize that hanging on by joining the governing coalition is merely a stopgap measure that does not provide a viable basis for political revival. In many ways, the tragedy of the Social Democrats has been the failure of coalescence in the labor movement to bring to pass a similar coalescence at the political level. Labor leader Akira Yamagishi had worked energetically for a decade to forge unity in the labor movement and to encourage reconciliation between the SDPJ and the DSP. During the fall of 1993, Yamagishi reportedly worked closely with Ozawa on behalf of the latter's political reform agenda because he hoped that the seven-party coalition might serve as a catalyst for such a reconciliation (Sato, Yoshio, 1993). This calculation collapsed with the fall of the Hosokawa government as the SDPJ and the DSP joined contending political camps. Soon thereafter, Yamagishi resigned as chairman of the labor organization Rengo in disgrace.

The fear of political extinction has provoked former SDPJ chairman Sadao Yamahana to take up the illusory objective of coalescing the so-called liberal and social democratic forces to form a political alternative to the two large conservative parties. The Hanshin earthquake in January 1995 derailed Yamahana's original plan to leave the SDPJ with his allies and form a new party.[2] Reformers in the Social Democratic Party now face an inexorable predicament. They can continue to clutch the temporary security of being a governing party only to face disastrous electoral results in the future. Or they can bolt the governing coalition sooner rather than later without any clear assurances that such a move will generate a revival of popular support. As Social Democratic leaders reflect upon their unattractive options, the power of organized labor in the political process will continue to decline.

Constitutionally, the next lower house election does not have to be held until the summer of 1997. But if there is a split in the government coalition or if LDP leaders feel ready to enter an electoral campaign under the new system, the prime minister could dissolve the House of Representatives sooner. The salient issues of the campaign are likely to be economic policies to deal with the recession and industrial restructuring, deregulation and administrative reform, responses to international pressures (especially from the United States) on trade and related matters, and social policies to deal with changes in the Japanese employment system. Security policy could emerge as a major issue if the North Korean nuclear problem has worsened or the North Korean regime is about to collapse, if the international community is looking to Japan to dispatch Self-Defense Forces in U.N. peacekeeping and peace enforcement missions in troubled areas like the former Yugoslavia, or if China appears to be undergoing a problematic leadership transition process.

---

[2]In May 1995, however, Yamahana and six other members of the SDPJ finally announced their intention to leave the party.

The July 1995 House of Councilors election has intensified public calls for an early lower house election. Not only did the SDPJ suffer a serious defeat, but also the Shinshinto surpassed the LDP in both the prefectural and proportional representation constituencies in terms of actual votes. More important, only 44.5 percent of the voters went to the polls, the lowest turnout rate in Japanese history for a national election. This rate suggests widespread public apathy and even disgust toward the existing political parties. The electoral success of the Shinshinto was largely the result of the Sokagakkai's ability to mobilize their members to go to the polls; it did not reflect a groundswell of citizen support for the Shinshinto. Although the pressure to dissolve the House of Representatives will mount, the upper house outcome has ironically reduced the LDP's incentive to hold a lower house election. Therefore, the timing of the next election will largely depend upon the intra-LDP conflicts that will inevitably emerge following the July 1995 electoral setback. A split in the LDP could bring down the current coalition, force an election, and trigger another round of political realignment. A decision by the SDPJ to leave the coalition to revitalize the party could also initiate a similar course of events.

Increase in Bureaucratic Power During Period of Political Fluidity

Given the fluidity of party politics, career bureaucrats, especially in the Ministry of Finance, are likely to exert more influence than usual on the details of policymaking. A *Nihon Keizai Shimbun* survey of House of Representatives members conducted in March–April 1994 revealed that 51 percent of the respondents felt that bureaucrats had become more powerful relative to politicians during this political transition period, while only 5 percent felt that politicians had become more powerful. Moreover, of the 265 representatives responding to the survey, an overwhelming majority of 170 felt that the influence of the Ministry of Finance had increased under the coalition government. Ten National Diet members believed that the power of the Ministry of Foreign Affairs (MOFA) had increased, while no one mentioned the Defense Agency as having become more powerful (*Nihon Keizai Shimbun*, April 13, 1994, p. 7). New ideas on foreign policy are likely to emerge from the various bureaucratic agencies and not from the political parties. At the same time, the bureaucrats strongly resist changes that weaken their power, such as certain deregulation measures.

In its recent reorganization, the Ministry of Foreign Affairs created the General Foreign Policy Bureau (Sogo Gaiko Seisaku Kyoku) to serve as the ministry's focal point for developing Japan's long-range diplomatic strategy. Because the bureau's leadership (including the director general) tends to be senior in service to other MOFA officials holding similar ranks, it is likely to be highly effective in forging a ministrywide consensus. The Defense Agency is now taking the lead in drafting a revised National Defense Program Outline. This document will articulate the basic principles and objectives of Japanese defense policy for the post–Cold War era. Given Japan's importance as an economic actor, the economic ministries will also exert considerable influence in foreign policy. Since the oil crises of the 1970s, the Ministry of International Trade and Industry (MITI) has felt that security policy is too important to be left up to the Ministry of Foreign Affairs and the Defense Agency. Consequently, in addition to traditional trade and industrial policy issues, MITI will rely upon its network of research organizations as well as its own internal bureaus to reflect upon critical strategic questions such as regional economic integration in the Asia-Pacific, stabilization and reform in the former Soviet Union, the problem of sustainable development, the tension between economic development and political liberalization, and the diffusion of military and dual-use technologies. The Ministry of Finance (MOF) and its affiliated research institutes will focus on international affairs primarily from the perspective of financial markets and exchange rates. But MOF will also be critical in matters related to macroeconomic policy coordination among the advanced industrial states, the allocation of funds for foreign economic assistance, and the size of the Japanese defense budget.

The next few years will be a period of intellectual ferment for the bureaucratic world. Numerous informal study groups as well as formal deliberative councils sponsored by the various ministries will tap the ideas of scholars, policy analysts, and journalists. But this intellectual ferment is unlikely to lead to major policy initiatives until the political situation becomes clearer. Without a strong political will, coordination and integration across the various bureaucratic perspectives will be next to impossible. For the time being, influential politicians will form their own study groups—many with the help of individual career bureaucrats with whom they have developed close personal ties. Some will publish books articulating their own visions of Japan's future and use them to enhance their political standing. Morihiro Hosokawa, Ichiro Ozawa, Michio Watanabe, Masayoshi Takemura, and Ryutaro Hashimoto (one of the up and coming leaders of the LDP) have already written such works.

Eventually, the initiative may shift from the bureaucrats to politicians. Once the political reform and realignment process yields a stable party system, the parties will become better organized and develop their own networks for policy analysis. To the degree that elections become more competitive under the new system, party platforms could assume greater influence not only in election campaigns, but also in the policymaking process. Political leaders may become more intrusive in the personnel decisions of the various ministries and agencies so as to promote those who support their views. And foreign policy issues may become the subject of meaningful public debates, and these debates may shape concrete policy decisions. But for all of this to happen, politicians will need to develop greater confidence in bureaucrats. Currently, much of the substantive debate on complex policy questions is shaped by career bureaucrats. Their networks in research institutions and the mass media are so extensive that it is virtually impossible for politicians to absorb and articulate policy ideas that are independent of the national bureaucracy. The only long-term solution to this shortcoming is the creation of a number of truly independent think tanks that have respected scholars and analysts who can develop policies alternative to those of the bureaucracy. Without such institutions, politicians are likely to remain meek in their debates with elite bureaucrats. And they are likely to revert back to the comfortable role of being brokers between bureaucrats and interest groups that is the hallmark of the so-called zoku (tribe) politics.

FUTURE SCENARIOS

The process of political realignment could yield the following types of party systems:

- Competition among three political forces
- Loose two-party system
- Fragmented multiparty system.

Competition Among Three Political Forces

Perhaps the most likely outcome is a competitive system involving three loose political clusters. They will probably consist of: (1) a traditional conservative cluster centered around the LDP or a successor group, (2) a renovationist cluster centered around the Shinshinto, and (3) a liberal-social democratic cluster that has the SDPJ and Sakigake at the core and various defectors from the JNP and DSP. In such a system, no cluster is likely to achieve a single-party majority. Consequently, the liberal-social democratic cluster could emerge as a pivotal player in coalition politics. The dynamic of such a competition will be centrist, although the policy fault lines will be unclear. If the liberal-social democratic cluster chooses to align with the LDP, the policy orientation will be very similar to the current LDP-SDPJ-Sakigake coalition. A coalition government between the LDP and the Shinshinto-led renovationist cluster is unlikely to appear unless the personal animosity toward Ozawa among many Liberal Democrats subsides. If such a coalition did emerge and did become stable, then this would mean a resurrection of the old LDP-dominant system.

Loose Two-Party System

A two-party system could emerge through two paths. One would be a solidification of the current alignment, which pits the LDP-SDPJ-Sakigake coalition against the Shinshinto. This alignment makes sense now because it reflects a personality rift between pro-Ozawa and anti-Ozawa forces. If Ozawa were to lose political influence or if critical policy issues were to supersede personality conflicts, this two-camp division is likely to disintegrate. The other path to a two-party system would involve a few more rounds of political fragmentation, realignment, and reaggregation. Gradually, two political forces would emerge based upon substantive policy and ideological differences. The most likely basis for such a bipolar split would be constitutional and security policy issues. One party or cluster of parties would support constitutional revision and a more proactive defense policy, whereas the other would stress nonmilitary ways to promote international security. There is also the possibility that domestic policy could define the basis of interparty competition. One candidate for such a split is the debate between small and big government (Masuzoe, 1994, pp. 120–122). Proponents of small government would stress the virtues of deregulation, decentralization, and tax reductions. Advocates of big government might emphasize the virtues of government regulations and state spending. But as in the case of security policy, differences about domestic policy now crosscut the current government-opposition divide. Clarification of political divisions along policy lines is likely to come only when Japan is forced to make hard choices—either because of an external crisis or because of a dramatic decline in economic fortunes.

Fragmented Multiparty System

Despite the electoral pressures to aggregate political forces under the new electoral system, crosscutting personality and policy conflicts could obstruct the formation of *stable* political alliances. The LDP could fragment as the internal factional system for managing intraparty conflict disintegrates. Even the SDPJ could split because of dissension on various policy questions. If personality conflicts prevent a reaggregation of political forces along policy lines, then the coalitions that form would be based upon short-term political opportunism. Governments would be unstable and weak and therefore unable to make hard choices to respond to various international as well as domestic challenges. Prolonged instability could eventually produce a vigorous nationalist right committed to restoring order and improving Japan's international stature.

Chapter Three

ECONOMIC TRANSFORMATION

Japan has been in the throes of one of the worst economic recessions since the end of World War II. Since 1988, the nation's annual growth rates in terms of real gross domestic product (GDP) have fallen sharply (see Figure 3.1). In 1993, Japan's GDP in real terms declined by 0.2 percent. This was the worst performance since 1974 when the GDP declined by 0.6 percent because of the first oil crisis. Although growth resumed in 1994, economic recovery remains weak. The recession of 1991–1993 has challenged the efficacy of economic

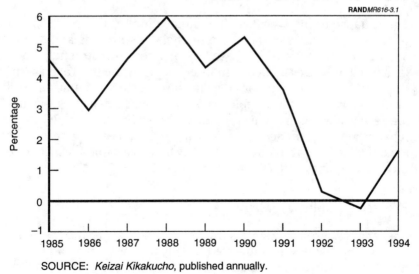

SOURCE: *Keizai Kikakucho*, published annually.

Figure 3.1—Japan's Annual Real GDP Growth Rate

policies and business practices that have served the country so well for nearly four decades. It may also affect the credibility and applicability of the so-called Japanese model of development in the post–Cold War era for other states. Even if Japan's economy fully recovers from the current recession, long-term growth rates are likely to be low. Although optimistic forecasts predict growth at about 3.5 percent per year, a more likely growth rate would be in the 2–3 percent range (Noland, 1994, p. 12).

CAUSES OF THE ECONOMIC RECESSION

The latest recession, which has been more structural than cyclical in nature, has several interrelated causes:

* Collapse of the bubble economy

* Excessive productive capacity

* Yen appreciation.

Collapse of the Bubble Economy

The collapse of the so-called "bubble economy" in early 1990 imposed severe strains on Japanese financial institutions and dampened consumer spending as well as business investment. Many Japanese banks are saddled with heavy debts, while the Tokyo securities market has seen a sharp decline in stock values. Japan will still be able to avoid an acute capital shortage because of its high savings rate, especially relative to its investment rate. This fact is reflected in Japan's large current account surplus. Nevertheless, Japanese firms are unlikely to enjoy access to relatively low-cost capital, which gave them a competitive edge in the past (Noguchi, 1993, pp. 19–47).

Excessive Productive Capacity

The Japanese economy suffers from overcapacity. During the boom years of the 1980s, Japan invested heavily in new plants and equipment. Now with a global economic downturn, Japanese firms are having great difficulty finding outlets for their surplus production. Consequently, they are having to downsize their productive capacity, including workforce reductions, while suffering major financial losses. Uncertainties about employment security have reinforced the decline in consumer confidence, further deepening the recession.

Yen Appreciation

Japan confronts an unfavorable trading environment. Yen appreciation has reduced the price competitiveness of Japanese goods relative to those produced by foreign firms. In terms of purchasing power parity (PPP), the yen is now extremely overvalued. According to estimates of Japan's Economic Planning Agency, the purchasing power parity is 115 yen to the dollar for tradable goods and 155 yen to the dollar for consumer goods (Suzuki, February 2–9, 1995, p. 3; Suzuki, April 1995, p. 6). This sharp appreciation of the yen is in part a reflection of Japan's huge current account surplus. In 1992, the current account balance in U.S. dollars reached an historic high of $130 billion. This surplus, which reflects the country's high savings rate, however, does not necessarily have to produce an overvalued yen. If Japan could quickly recycle abroad its surplus dollars earned through foreign trade, then the upward pressure on the yen would not be as great as it has been in the spring of 1995. Unfortunately, problems in the financial sector have constricted the recycling process. Moreover, with declining profits and increasing restructuring costs, Japanese multinational corporations are now more inclined to convert their dollar trade earnings into yen. This behavior has fueled the yen appreciation.

The weak economic recovery in both the United States and Western Europe has also made it difficult for Japan to export its way out of its recession as it had in the past. The danger of exacerbating economic tensions has foreclosed the possibility of making further inroads into the American and European markets. In fact, political pressures in the United States are mounting to get Japan to reduce its bilateral trade surplus as well as to liberalize its own market. Not only is it politically and economically impossible for Japan to pursue a strategy of export-led recovery, Japan's current international economic profile is becoming less tolerable in the eyes of the other advanced industrial states. Consequently, Japan now faces the formidable challenge of importing more foreign goods just as its business sector is struggling to make structural adjustments at home.

DEBATE ABOUT ECONOMIC POLICY

Ever since the high growth era that began in the 1960s, Japan's economic policy regime has had three features. First, government agencies cooperated with big business to enhance the international competitiveness of strategic industrial sectors. Market-conforming policy instruments nurtured new technologies, ensured stable domestic markets, mitigated the negative effects of "excessive competition," and promoted exports. As Japan became a first-rank industrial power, the more heavy-handed government measures for shaping industrial development gradually receded. A subtle, yet significant shift occurred from "state-guided industrialization" to what many have called "network capitalism." This form of capitalism involves constant consultations and cooperation between the economic ministries and the mainstream corporations to manage market trends both domestically and internationally. While generally consistent with market economics, this brand of capitalism has tended to privilege established large firms over new business entrants, to condone preferential trading practices among firms in a particular *keiretsu* (business network), and to accept de facto cartelization of many industries (Okimoto, 1989; Calder, 1993; Gerlach, 1992).

Second, while promoting internationally competitive sectors, the Japanese government has compensated the economically weak sectors like agriculture and small business, especially the retail sector. This compensatory policy has taken the form of import quotas and tariffs, price supports, direct and indirect subsidies, tax breaks, and protective regulations. The main aim of these measures was to prevent rapid industrial change from aggravating socioeconomic inequality and causing uneven development. In short, the Japanese have been willing to sacrifice economic efficiency and aggregate productivity gains to the extent necessary to sustain societal cohesion (Calder, 1988). This general policy orientation has had the support of not only the conservative Liberal Democratic Party, but also the opposition parties of the left and center.

Third, Japan's postwar economic policy regime has entailed an accommodation with organized labor. After nearly two decades of contentious labor-management relations, a modus vivendi between labor and management was achieved in both the private and public sectors during the mid-1960s. The labor movement focused increasingly on economic objectives such as employment security and wage increases while treating political objectives (e.g., abrogation of the U.S.-Japan Security Treaty) in increasingly ritualistic and symbolic terms. Enterprise unions, and not industrial unions, became the most important unit of labor organization. Nevertheless, the labor movement partially succeeded in overcoming the disadvantages of enterprise unionism by engaging in nationally coordinated "spring struggles" (*Shunto*). During the early 1970s, these struggles paid off in terms of significant annual wage increases that kept up with productivity increases. But from organized labor's perspective, the most important aspect of the implicit social contract between business and labor was employment security for "regular" workers. Unions tended to accept industrial rationalization measures and even wage restraints as long as their members continued to enjoy "lifetime employment." There was an understanding in Japanese corporate life that any breach of this norm would require management to compensate workers through employment opportunities in subsidiaries or related companies and/or hefty retirement awards (Hiwatari, 1991, pp. 87–140; Garon and Mochizuki, 1993).

This political economy based upon government-business cooperation and consultations, compensation for weak economic sectors, and accommodation with labor made it possible for Japan to respond effectively to changes in world markets and technology while minimizing the dislocative effects on domestic society due to the "creative destruction" of capitalism. Japanese-style capitalism involved more than what Chalmers Johnson has called the "developmental state." It was a form of developmental corporatism involving a consensus forged among government, political parties, and the key societal groups. While "developmental corporatism" benefited Japan enormously, the problem was that it tended to export the social costs of economic adjustments to Japan's more liberal trading partners, especially the United States.

With the end of the Cold War, however, developmental corporatism has come under severe challenges. Yen appreciation is making it much more costly to sustain the preferential trading practices among *keiretsu* firms. The United States is becoming much more aggressive about increasing access to Japanese markets. And given rapid technological changes in such areas as telecommunications, government regulations appear to be obstructing positive industrial development led by private sector initiative. In this context, a vigorous debate has emerged among Japanese government officials and policy analysts around the following general policy issues:

- Expansionary fiscal policy
- Changes in tax policy
- Economic deregulation.

Expansionary Fiscal Policy

At the macroeconomic level, Japan must find a way of stimulating domestic demand without throwing its public finances awry. Since Japan has been relatively successful in reducing its public debt during the 1980s and enjoys a large trade surplus, other advanced industrial countries, especially the United States, are looking to Japan to play a greater role in stimulating worldwide economic growth. There is also a strong domestic constituency for demand stimulation, especially from business and labor organizations. Both MOFA and MITI have joined this call for a looser fiscal policy. The main resistance to such a response is the fiscally conservative MOF.

MOF opposes a major stimulus package without solid assurance that the government will be able to raise the revenue to compensate for the spending increases. The last thing they want to do is to repeat the experience of the early 1970s during which MOF agreed to an expansionary fiscal policy that triggered double-digit inflation and a rapid accumulation of public debt. MOF officials point out ad nauseam that the aging of Japan's population will reduce the government's revenue base while expanding public expenditures in social programs. Therefore, the nation's long-term fiscal health depends upon controlling the temptation of deficit financing. The seriousness of the latest recession, however, did compel even the fiscally conservative MOF bureaucrats to announce four stimulus packages between August 1992 and February 1994, which totaled ¥45.4 trillion or approximately $454 billion (calculated at a ¥100 to $1.00 exchange rate). But in many respects, these initiatives were primarily public relations gimmicks. The revised budgets added very little new spending. The stimulus packages consisted largely of existing spending and loan programs that had been temporally rearranged, projected decreases in taxes, and loan guarantees.

The basic problem that Japan faces in terms of macroeconomic policy is the structural asymmetry between public finance and private capital. Despite the collapse of the bubble economy, Japan still is a capital surplus country as reflected in its large current account surplus. But given the low rate of taxation relative to other advanced industrial countries, the government has limited ability to soak up this capital surplus and direct it toward public spending to stimulate the economy without risking rapid debt accumulation. A significant portion of Japanese private savings has been in the postal savings system and the various government pension schemes. These funds have in turn been channeled into the Fiscal Investment and Loan Program (FILP). Although the government originally distributed the FILP funds to help finance Japan's industrial reconstruction and development, the government now uses these funds to support a variety of social projects (e.g., public housing, educational facilities, welfare programs, road development, etc.) (Reading, 1992, pp. 145–147). While the government has used the FILP as a fiscal stimulus instrument in recent years, the MOF appears reluctant to expand this use of the FILP. The involvement of numerous high government officials and construction industry executives in bribery and bid-rigging scandals has also restrained the use of public works spending to reinvigorate the economy.

Changes in Tax Policy

As a supplement or even an alternative to public spending increases, a number of influential Japanese economists proposed a major income tax cut to stimulate the economy. But the MOF adamantly opposed such a measure unless there was some guarantee that a hike in the consumption tax would be implemented in the near future to meet the revenue shortfall once the economy got back on track. In effect, the issues of an income tax reduction and a consumption tax increase become politically linked. Moreover, fiscal conservatives used the tax issue, which was originally raised to deal with the recession, to reinject the long-term problem of an aging society into the national agenda. Through a consumption tax hike, they hoped to put Japanese public finances on a secure footing to cope with the inevitable increase in social spending as the nation's demographic profile shifted toward the elderly. Leading politicians like Ichiro Ozawa of the Shinshinto and Yoshiro Mori of the Liberal Democratic Party embraced this linkage between the income tax cut and the consumption tax hike ("Zeisei kaikaku," 1993). And in November 1993, the Government Investigative Commission on the Tax System endorsed this combination. Critics of this linkage pointed out that any stimulative effect of an income tax cut would be diluted by the dampening effect of a prospective consumption tax hike. In the end, a compromise was worked out after the formation of the LDP-SDPJ-Sakigake government. The three-party coalition extended by one-year the 20 percent cut in personal income taxes. But at the same time, it enacted an increase of the consumption tax from 3 to 5 percent. Although this hike will not take effect until 1997, the MOF succeeded in getting National Diet approval for the rate increase and steering the country from a reliance on direct taxation to indirect taxation.

All of this indicates that there is widespread resistance in Japan to deficit financing as a countercyclical policy instrument on its own terms. But what could emerge out of this current recession is a structural transformation of public finances so that the government has a broader and deeper revenue base. Some economists believe that a higher rate of consumption taxes and a general shift from direct to indirect taxation will help to soak up some of the excess personal savings and channel these resources toward social investments to improve the quality of life in Japan (Nakatani, 1993). Not only would such a policy change help to reduce Japan's current account surplus, it would also reduce Japan's relative investment in productive capacity, which has fueled its aggressive export drive. As a result, Japan's economic profile would become more harmonious with the rest of the advanced industrial world.

Although the MOF enthusiastically supports the idea of shifting from direct to indirect taxation, it is not so keen about pursuing proactive policies to reduce the relative weight of savings in Japan's macroeconomic profile. First of all, the ministry believes that Japan's high savings rate will naturally decline as its population ages. Regarding the macroeconomic imbalance between Japan and the United States, they view the problem as the low savings rate in the United States, not the high savings rate in Japan. In other words, MOF officials argue, why should Japan drastically alter its macroeconomic policies to accommodate the United States, which has pursued misguided macroeconomic policies for so many years? At the macroeconomic level, it is the United States, not Japan, that must do more of the changing. According to one senior MOF official, the efforts at correcting the U.S.-Japan macroeconomic imbalance have been one-sided. "At the time of dollar depreciation, when Japan engaged in expanding domestic demand, the United States should have reduced its federal deficit and tightened its monetary policy to correct the imbalances. But instead the United States did the exact opposite" (Gyoten, 1993, pp. 157–158). Secondly, some in the MOF believe that chronic Japanese current account surpluses may not necessarily be a bad thing. Such surpluses could facilitate Japan's playing a more active role in international affairs (Farnsworth, 1990).

Economic Deregulation

At the microeconomic level, economic deregulation has been one of the top policy priorities of every government since the end of one-party LDP rule in 1993. Prime Minister Hosokawa personally trumpeted deregulation as the way to inject new vitality into the economy as well as to satisfy U.S. and other foreign pressures for greater economic transparency and openness. His successor, Tsutomu Hata also pledged to promote deregulation and decentralization. Even Prime Minister Murayama has publicly committed his government to pursue deregulation. Indeed the general call for deregulation has garnered widespread support in the mass media and among influential economists (Kisei Kanwa Kenkyukai, 1994; Rinji Gyosei Kaikaku Suishin Shingikai Jimushitsu, 1989; Tajima, 1994). Economic commentators insist that extensive deregulation is essential to facilitate the necessary adjustments in Japanese industrial structure and to make the services sector more competitive. But when it comes to concrete action, bureaucratic and interest group resistance remains strong.

In March 1995, the Murayama government released its long awaited five-year regulatory reform program. Japanese business leaders as well as the U.S. government reacted to this package with strong disappointment. Although the initiative contained more than 1,000 measures for deregulation, most of them were just warmed-over proposals that had been previously announced. For many of the important items, the government did not specify clear timetables for implementation. While the reform program endorsed the notion that state regulation should be the exception and not the norm, it did not commit the government to review all of the over 10,000 regulations currently in force. State pricing regulations in major industries such as airlines, telecommunications, and non–life insurance will remain in force, thereby sustaining de facto cartels. And there was no commitment to review the Large Retail Store Law, which impedes a transformation of the retail sector so that foreign goods will be more available to consumers. One of the problems with the deregulation drive has been the fluid state of politics and the weak leadership of the present coalition government. As a consequence, the task of drafting concrete measures has fallen upon the bureaucrats themselves. Since bureaucrats were behind the adoption of most of the regulations in the first place, it is not surprising that they would be reluctant deregulators. Given that regulations help to maintain bureaucratic power, there is little incentive for bureaucrats to vigorously push a reform program that would ultimately undercut their authority.

Despite all the disappointment, one positive development has come out of the latest cycle of deregulation. The March 1995 initiative mandated an annual review-revision process that solicits feedback and recommendations from the private sector. Moreover, the government has committed itself to issue yearly deregulation white papers that will evaluate state regulatory schemes in a comprehensive manner as well as evaluate the impact of deregulation. Even though concrete results may be long in coming, the transparency of the state regulatory process is likely to improve. And greater transparency could facilitate a more thoroughgoing deregulation program when a more vigorous political force for reform emerges.

While deregulation proceeds slowly at the policy level, Japanese consumers have been pushing for substantial changes in retailing. The prolonged recession coupled with a growing awareness of the domestic-foreign price differential has turned the Japanese into bargain hunters. Supermarket chains like Daiei are slashing prices to attract shoppers. Discount stores have sprouted in remote areas to dodge the restrictive regulations on opening large-scale stores. This new generation of retailers is taking advantage of yen appreciation and circumventing traditional distribution networks to offer customers lower prices without the intense personal service and after-sales support provided by older stores (Keizai Kikakucho, 1994). This revolution in retailing and consumer behavior does provide an opportunity for foreign producers to sell more of their goods in Japan. But a large part of the increased sales in these discount retailers may be products manufactured by Japanese corporate affiliates in low-cost labor countries, especially those located in Southeast Asia and southern China.

EFFECT ON INDUSTRIAL STRUCTURE AND THE LABOR MARKET

While political elites debate the most appropriate response to the current economic recession, market forces are transforming the economic landscape of Japan. To correct the overinvestments of the 1980s, most Japanese firms will reduce their productive capacities and even their workforce. Ultimately, this structural adjustment process will manifest itself in the following ways:

- Changes in *keiretsu* and subcontracting relationships
- Labor market fluidity
- Increase in foreign workers.

Changes in *Keiretsu* and Subcontracting Relationships

Yen appreciation and the internationalization of production are beginning to change *keiretsu* subcontracting relationships. Because of higher costs and lower profits, many large firms are having to reduce the number of suppliers and even to cut back their orders with favored subcontractors. Some consolidation of subcontracting networks could proceed as big manufacturers (e.g., in the automotive industry) become less reluctant to source from suppliers outside their traditional networks to reduce costs. At the same time, to survive, the subcontractors are likely to seek business opportunities with a wide variety of large firms, including those with rival *keiretsu*.

Cost-cutting pressures are also likely to increase the amount of cross-*keiretsu* trading.

Despite these changes, it is far from clear that Japanese corporations will shift away from a network-style to an auction-based capitalism where price becomes the main factor in sourcing production inputs. At the margins, firms will want to take advantage of yen appreciation and lower labor costs by buying more from foreign-based suppliers. Nevertheless, the Japanese will continue to place priority on familiarity and reliability over simple price calculations. Numerous studies by economists have recently appeared arguing how these traditional practices have clear economic benefits (Aoki, 1990). Therefore, to the extent that companies source from abroad, they will turn to subcontractors with which they have developed longer term relationships through joint ventures or other mechanisms. They will also have an incentive to encourage offshore investments of their traditional supplier networks. To quote from the prominent Japanese economist, Dr. Yoshio Suzuki, "profit maximization in a market economy takes longer in East Asia than in the West. Also, fair competition in a market does not necessarily mean equal opportunity in spot transactions, and sometimes it can mean equal opportunity in long-term relationships with good customers" (Suzuki, February 2–9, 1995).

Labor Market Fluidity

Despite the media attention given to firm layoffs and the creeping increase in unemployment, it is highly unlikely that Japan will experience intense labor unrest comparable to the 1950s. This adjustment process comes at a time when the Japanese labor market has been tight for many years. Consequently, unlike West European countries, Japan ought to be able to absorb the layoffs with minimal negative social and political effects. The unemployment rate has gone up from 2.1 percent in 1990 to 3.2 percent in April 1995. The more pessimistic forecasts see unemployment rising above 4 percent. For young people entering the labor force (those aged 15 to 24), the rate is now in the 6 percentile range (Pollack, 1995). Even so, compared with other advanced industrial democracies, Japan's unemployment problem will still be mild.

The long-term trend in the Japanese labor market is that of labor scarcity, not labor abundance (Yashiro, 1995). According to one economist, while the Japanese labor force grew at a rate of 0.92 percent in 1980–1990, the growth rate will decline to 0.36 percent over the decade 1990–2000. In the following decade of 2000–2010, the labor force is likely to shrink at a rate of 0.35 percent per year (Bauer, 1990). The aging of Japan's population over the next two decades will not only dramatically raise government social policy expenditures, but also push wage costs upward for private corporations. With this trend in mind, large Japanese firms have already adapted by reducing the importance of seniority for wage calculations (Clark and Ogawa, 1992). By weakening the incentive for workers to stay in one company for most of one's career, this change in the wage structure could enhance the fluidity of the labor market and encourage employees to seek better job opportunities in expanding sectors.

In the short to medium term, however, there will be a labor surplus problem centering around white-collar employees, not industrial workers (Chuma, 1994). Up until now, to deal with excess white-collar workers, companies tended to transfer mid-level managers to subsidiaries and affiliated firms. Low economic growth may make such a response more difficult. Deregulation could create opportunities to start up new businesses in promising sectors such as information services and thereby help to absorb redundant white-collar workers. But at the same time, deregulation could also increase layoffs by forcing firms to become more efficient, especially at the managerial and clerical levels.

Thus far, the most visible impact of the economic slowdown has been on the hiring of college graduates entering the regular job market for the first time. Only a few years ago, these young graduates enjoyed multiple job offers. Now as firms struggle to minimize layoffs of their so-called "permanent" workers, they are reluctant to hire new employees. Hiring reductions and even freezes in many of the blue-ribbon companies have intensified the job competition for young people and forced many well-qualified candidates to pursue less-traditional career tracks. Those who are successful in landing a good job are likely to face salary freezes.

Increase in Foreign Workers

The labor issue that could provoke the greatest political difficulty in the long run is the problem of foreign workers. Unlike West European countries, Japan resisted for a long time the use of foreign workers to deal with its labor shortage. The Labor Ministry wanted to maximize employment opportunities for Japanese nationals and to minimize the negative social effects of labor immigration. Major corporations preferred to utilize labor-saving production techniques, rather than hire foreigners. But the high value of the yen now makes working in Japan especially attractive to people from South and Southeast Asia and Latin America. Cost-cutting pressures also give Japanese small firm owners a strong incentive to hire such workers at low wages and with little employment security. The industries most affected by the labor shortage are service establishments, small-scale manufacturing, and construction. By the year 2000, Japan could face a shortage of about 1 million workers (Oka, 1994). Moreover, because most Japanese are now reluctant to take jobs that are *kiken* (dangerous), *kitanai* (dirty), and *kitsui* (difficult), employment opportunities for non-Japanese have increased dramatically.

Although Japan has yet to develop a comprehensive policy regarding foreign workers, a large number of foreigners who have entered on student or tourist visas have chosen to stay in Japan and earn good yen-based wages. The government is gingerly experimenting with different policies. One program provides extended stays to foreigners of Japanese ancestry under the rationale that they are visiting relatives. In reality, most of them work in designated communities. Official estimates are that over 500,000 nonpermanent resident foreigners are now working in Japan. Of these, over 200,000 are believed to be working illegally. Only about 150,000 fall under the program for those of Japanese ancestry (Kosai and Shigeo, 1993, pp. 129–130).

As Japanese workers themselves face layoffs while some jobs go to foreign workers, one can imagine the rise of nationalistic antiforeign movements similar to those that have arisen in Germany. But the more important issue will be the social implications. Japan's homogeneous population and general wariness of outsiders makes assimilation of foreign workers extremely difficult (Kajita, 1994). Criminal or other incidents involving foreigners will reinforce this suspicion.

On the other hand, the cold reception given to foreign workers (especially those of non-European descent) at the community level could intensify their frustrations about living in a country like Japan with clear social boundaries between insiders and outsiders. Tensions between Japanese and foreigners could then arouse a xenophobic reaction from Japanese as well as provoke international criticisms.

IMPLICATIONS FOR FOREIGN TRADE AND INVESTMENTS

Japan's domestic economic transformation has the following external economic implications:

- Deepening of Japan's economic linkages with East Asia

- Weakening of U.S. economic leverage in the region.

Deepening of Japan's Economic Linkages with East Asia

For both economic and political reasons, Japanese firms no longer see the United States as the most attractive country for expanding exports or direct investments. While trying to sustain their market shares in the advanced industrial nations, they will focus on the transfer of production facilities to East Asian countries to take advantage of lower labor costs and growing markets (Lincoln, 1993, pp. 160–200). During the second half of the 1980s, Japanese foreign direct investments (FDI) into North America and Western Europe rose more steeply than investments into East Asia (see Figure 3.2). After 1989, Japanese foreign direct investments declined precipitously, especially to North America and Western Europe. But in 1991–1992, investments into East Asia began to increase, while investments into the other two regions continued to fall. The passage of the North American Free Trade Agreement (NAFTA), however, could kindle some Japanese business interest in investments in Mexico to maintain access to U.S. and Canadian markets.

Although Figure 3.2 suggests that the United States and Canada continue to be the primary targets of Japanese direct investments, a closer look reveals a somewhat different picture. In 1993, 55.1 percent of Japan's direct investment in East Asia was in manufacturing,

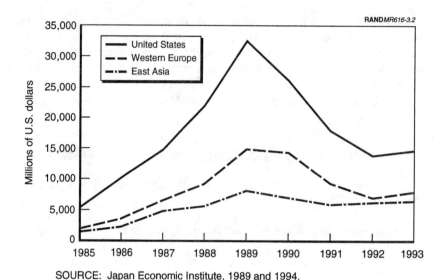

SOURCE: Japan Economic Institute, 1989 and 1994.

NOTE: East Asia refers to the East Asian Newly Industrializing Economies (South Korea, Taiwan, Hong Kong, and Singapore), the ASEAN Four (Thailand, Malaysia, the Philippines, and Indonesia), and China.

Figure 3.2—Japan's Foreign Direct Investments

whereas only 27.1 percent of its direct investment in North America was in this sector (Moriguchi, 1995). Therefore, Japanese annual FDI in manufacturing in East Asia is approaching parity with comparable FDI in the United States. Before long, Japanese firms will place much more emphasis on East Asia, rather than North America, as a production base. From the regional perspective, the trend is more pronounced. Despite increased American business interest in East Asia, Japan is outinvesting the United States by a wide margin. In the 1990–1993 period, Japan's FDI in the rest of East Asia totaled about $26 billion, while comparable American FDI to non-Japan East Asia was approximately $15 billion (Mason, 1994, p. 31). In recent years, the character as well as quantity of Japanese investments have changed. Rather than large firms merely setting up assembly facilities to reap the benefits of cheap labor, Japanese business networks are now promoting the outward investment of small affiliated subcontractors. In effect, Japan is expanding its production networks

throughout the region. Although this investment pattern has facili-
tated the development of the host economies, it has also made these
economies more dependent upon Japanese management skills, ma-
chinery, and technology (Bernard and Ravenhill, 1995; Dobson,
1993).

In terms of foreign trade, the East Asian region as a whole is now a
larger trading partner than the United States for Japan. Two-way
trade with East Asia surpassed that with the United States in 1990
(see Figure 3.3). Japan now exports more to East Asia than to either
the United States or Western Europe (see Figure 3.4).

These trade figures, however, do not support the view that Japan may
be developing a self-contained regional economic system. The
United States continues to be the primary absorber of both Japanese
and East Asian exports, while Japan has a large trade surplus with
both the United States and the East Asia region (see Figure 3.5 and
3.6). The only two East Asian economies with which Japan has a
trade deficit are China and Indonesia. Moreover, Japan will continue to invest in the United States to maintain access not only to
America's large consumer market, but also to America's high technologies.

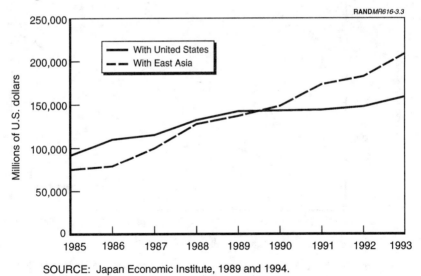

SOURCE: Japan Economic Institute, 1989 and 1994.

Figure 3.3—Japan's Two-Way Trade with the United States and East Asia

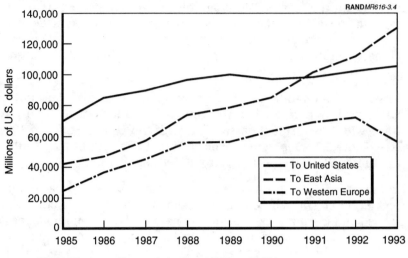

SOURCE: Japan Economic Institute, 1989 and 1994.

Figure 3.4—Japan's Exports to the United States, East Asia, and Western Europe

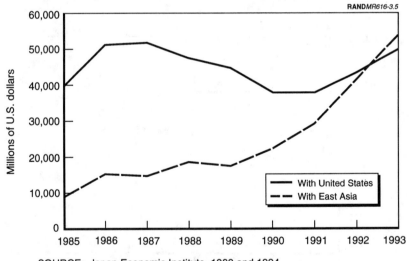

SOURCE: Japan Economic Institute, 1989 and 1994.

Figure 3.5—Japan's Trade Balance with East Asia and the United States

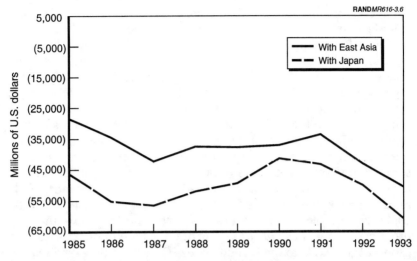

SOURCE: Japan Economic Institute, 1989 and 1994.

NOTE: Amounts in parentheses represent a trade deficit.

Figure 3.6—U.S. Trade Balance with East Asia and Japan

The deepening of Japanese economic linkages with East Asia could challenge the United States in two ways. First, although Japan is not creating a self-contained regional economic bloc under its leadership, the expansion of its business networks may make it increasingly difficult for American businesses to tap the region's economic dynamism. This is not to imply that the East Asian region is not large enough for both Japanese and American businesses. The region, of course, is large enough. But given the high value of the yen, the lower cost and greater availability of Japanese investment capital, and the intricacy of Japanese business networks, U.S. companies may have difficulty competing with their Japanese counterparts in East Asian markets.

Second, the trade flows among Japan, East Asia, and the United States pose a difficult political problem. While continuing to post large trade surpluses with the United States, Japan is enhancing the productive capacity of the developing economies in East Asia through exports of equipment and intermediate products as well as capital. The East Asian economies, in turn, are exporting their excess production mainly to the United States. Although Japanese imports from East Asia have risen steadily since the mid-1980s, they still lag far behind U.S. imports from East Asia. By "exporting" export-led development to other East Asian countries, Japan is posing a trade challenge both directly (Japanese exports) and indirectly (non-Japanese East Asian exports). This does not mean that Japan is simply creating "export platforms" in East Asia that are directed to the American market. Evidence from empirical research suggests that a significant portion of the production from Japanese manufacturing investments goes to serve the local and regional markets. And some of the output gets exported back to Japan. Moreover, studies have shown that American firms investing abroad may be more likely to export back to the United States (Graham and Anzai, 1994; Urata, 1993). Nevertheless, to pay for the imports of Japanese intermediate products, many of the East Asian economies are under pressure to export aggressively to the United States. Otherwise they could face a severe current account deficit problem.

Of course, East Asian economic growth does benefit the United States in terms of expanding export markets and cheaper imports (especially consumer goods). But the huge influx of imports from Japan and other East Asian economies poses formidable adjustment challenges for U.S. business sectors that must compete with these Asian imports. Moreover, because U.S. trade with East Asia is more likely to be inter-industry rather than intra-industry in character, America's large trade deficit with East Asia as a whole is likely to politicize trade relations. U.S. industries that are hurt by imports will use the political process to seek protectionist relief, and American trade officials will be more aggressive in pressing the East Asian countries to liberalize their economic policies and business practices. More Japanese absorption of East Asian imports would mitigate some of this trade pressure on the U.S. economy, but this is unlikely until a political force with both the will and power emerges in Japan to stimulate domestic demand. A continuation of the current regional trade patterns could have important consequences for interstate relations. Since the United States and most of the East Asian economies have large trade deficits with Japan, one might expect American and East Asian cooperation to get Japan to facilitate foreign access to its markets. But because the United States has trade deficits with both Japan and many of the East Asian economies,

Washington might be tempted to pursue aggressive trade liberalization policies that might bring Tokyo and the other East Asian capitals
closer together.

Weakening of U.S. Economic Leverage in the Region

Given current trends, U.S. economic leverage in the region is likely to
decline for the following reasons. First, even while the East Asian
trade surplus with the United States is growing, intra-East Asian
trade is also expanding. As U.S. business interest in East Asian export
markets increases in the context of growing intra-East Asian trade, an
American threat to restrict access to its own markets is likely to be
less effective in winning trade concessions.

Second, the ability of the United States to mobilize the support of the
East Asian countries to pressure Japan to open its markets will
diminish. Right now, Japan has a great deal of leverage over the
developing economies in the region because of its huge foreign aid
programs. By contrast, the United States provides only a negligible
amount of aid to East Asia. As more and more East Asian countries
graduate from their status as developing economies, Japanese aid
will inevitably become a less powerful instrument for wielding
regional influence. Nevertheless, Japan will remain the single most
important source of private capital and technology in the region.
With the expansion of Japanese business networks throughout the
region and the growing incorporation of local suppliers into these
networks, East Asian governments will be hard pressed to turn
against Japanese interests in an alliance with the United States.

Finally, the internationalization of the yen as the currency for regional economic transactions could strengthen Japanese influence
while reducing America's. Although most analysts see the emergence
of a yen bloc in East Asia as being far-fetched, yen internationalization is likely to accelerate (Frankel, 1993). The rapid increase of Japanese trade with East Asian countries due to regional
growth and expansion of regional Japanese FDI will increase the use
of the yen as an invoice currency. In the context of yen appreciation
coupled with the large amounts of Japanese aid being provided in
yen-denominated loans, central banks in East Asian countries will
have an incentive to increase the amount of yen in their foreign exchange reserves. And to the extent that developing countries in the

region are successful in exporting more to Japan, the growth of yen receipts will inevitably expand the use of the yen as a reserve currency (Noland, 1994, p. 37). These factors will enhance Japan's independence from the United States in terms of monetary policy as well as exchange rate fluctuations.

Chapter Four

ATTITUDINAL CHANGE

ELITE AND INTELLECTUAL OPINION

Three trends stand out in elite and intellectual opinion:

- Sharpened debate among mainstream security policy analysts: great power internationalism versus civilian internationalism

- Growing critiques of Japan's past approach to economic development

- The Rise of a "New Asianism."

Sharpened Debate Among Mainstream Security Policy Analysts: Great Power Internationalism Versus Civilian Internationalism

During the Cold War era, the debate among intellectuals and specialists regarding Japanese security policy basically involved three schools of thought. Nationalists on the right argued that Japan should revise its postwar constitution to permit unencumbered rearmament (including the acquisition of power projection capabilities) and should pursue a foreign policy less dependent upon the United States. Pacifists on the left advocated strict adherence to the pacifist principles embodied in the constitution and a policy of unarmed neutralism. Mainstream analysts supported the government's policy of interpreting the constitution so as to permit defensive military forces and to permit maintenance of the security relationship with the United States.

The twin shocks of the Persian Gulf crisis of 1990–1991 and the collapse of the Soviet Union have fundamentally transformed the above debate. Proponents of neutralism and a strictly pacifist foreign policy have waned in influence because of a growing recognition that Japan must assume more of the responsibilities and burdens of maintaining international security commensurate with its economic capabilities. Nationalistic advocates of "great power autonomy" continue to attract much attention, especially among the foreign press, but their impact on Japanese security policy continues to be limited. The salient debate with concrete policy implications is now among mainstream analysts and involves two forms of internationalism: "great power internationalism" and "civilian internationalism." Both schools of thought are internationalist in the sense that they support maintaining good relations with the United States and pursuing Japan's national interests in cooperation with the major powers of the West. But they differ in terms of the appropriate modalities of such international cooperation.

The great power internationalists would like Japan to assume military responsibilities commensurate with its economic power to revitalize the alliance with the United States for the post–Cold War era. Although the security partnership with the United States would be pivotal, the great power internationalists also envisage Japan participating in a "great power concert" of advanced industrial democracies for maintaining a stable global security order.[1] They embrace the following policy agenda:

- Expansion of host-nation support for U.S. forces in Japan both in monetary and substantive terms (e.g., financial contributions for fuel used by American aircraft), and financial contributions to help defray the cost of maintaining U.S. forces in the Pacific, not just in Japan.

- Cooperation with U.S. forces for military operations in the Asia-Pacific region beyond defense of the Japanese archipelago, and

---

[1]Prominent great power internationalists include Hisahiko Okazaki, Seizaburo Sato, and Masashi Nishihara. See Okazaki, 1994; and Nakasone, Sato, Murakami, and Nishibe, 1992, pp. 165–229.

reinterpretation and even revision of the U.S.-Japan Security Treaty to mandate a broader regional security role for Japan.

• Promotion of defense technological cooperation with the United States (e.g., the joint development of a theater-missile-defense system).

• Legislation to permit the dispatch of Self-Defense Forces overseas to rescue Japanese citizens.

• Active participation in U.N. peacekeeping operations (including the assumption of combat missions), the establishment of regional training centers for such operations, and eventually full participation in U.N. peace enforcement operations and permanent membership for Japan in the U.N. Security Council.

• Reinterpretation and even revision of the Constitution not only to legitimate explicitly the Self-Defense Forces, but also to affirm the right of collective security and defense.

Certain aspects of this agenda were articulated in a soft-pedaled manner in the report drafted by the Liberal Democratic Party's Commission on Contributions to International Society in the wake of the Persian Gulf crisis. Ichiro Ozawa chaired this group. Ozawa has developed these ideas further in his book *Nihon Kaizo Keikaku* [Plan for the Restructuring of Japan] and invoked the notion of becoming a normal country to justify his views. Of the mainstream press, the *Yomiuri Shimbun* has increasingly supported views similar to great power internationalism. In 1992, the newspaper organized a study council on the postwar constitution that recommended enacting a "Basic Law for Security" to legitimate and clarify Japan's individual and collective right to self-defense (The Yomiuri Constitution Study Council, 1992).

"Civilian internationalists" believe that Japan should build upon its post–World War II pacifistic tradition and contribute to world affairs primarily through nonmilitary means by becoming a "global civilian power." Although this school of thought has not articulated a vision that is as clear and geopolitically compelling as Ozawa's normal-country concept, it does have greater support among the Japanese people.[2] The policy agenda of civilian internationalism includes the following:

- Adherence to a strictly defensive military doctrine, and reduction in the rate of defense spending increases.

- Active participation in and promotion of arms control processes both regionally and globally.

- Explicit acknowledgment of Japan's imperialist past to foster greater trust among Asian countries toward Japan, while championing human rights and democratization in the region.

- Promotion of regional economic integration as a way to mitigate geopolitical distrust among East Asian countries.

- Contribution to international security primarily through non-military means (e.g., foreign aid, humanitarian relief, and non-combat peacekeeping roles), and development of a foreign policy that is less focused on economic interests and more supportive of other themes such as environmental protection.

- Efforts to strengthen multilateral institutions (e.g., the United Nations) while refraining from pressing the issue of permanent membership in the U.N. Security Council.

Both Morihiro Hosokawa and Masayoshi Takemura have written books embracing many aspects of civilian internationalism. In fact, Takemura's recent work *Chisaku tomo kirari to hikaru kuni: Nihon* [Japan: A Small But Sparkling Country] was clearly written to counter Ozawa's notion of a normal country (Takemura, 1994). Given the security policy differences among the political parties that participated in both Hosokawa's "seven plus one" coalition government and Murayama's three-party coalition, the intellectual debate between great power internationalism and civilian internationalism will be a key factor in shaping the political realignment process.

---

[2]Proponents of civilian internationalism include Yoichi Funabashi of the *Asahi Shimbun* and Takehiko Kamo of Tokyo University. See Funabashi, 1993; and Kamo, 1993.

Growing Critiques of Japan's Past Approach to Economic Development

The dominant intellectual paradigm to explain Japan's political economy and economic performance in the postwar period can probably be summed up as "developmental corporatism." As many Japanese and American scholars have argued, the Japanese state and the business sector have worked together to develop strategic industries and enhance international economic competitiveness (Johnson, 1982; Okimoto, 1989; and Murakami, 1987). But along with this probusiness developmentalism, Japan protected and compensated economic sectors such as agriculture and small business (and to some extent labor) to sustain a social consensus in favor of rapid economic growth and to ease the pain of adjustment to market forces (Calder, 1988). In short, developmentalism drove Japanese firms to aggressively expand into foreign markets, while corporatist policies and practices at home made it difficult for foreign firms to penetrate the Japanese market. Although developmental corporatism served Japan well while it was seeking to "catch up" economically with the West and in particular the United States, most Japanese intellectuals and opinion leaders now recognize the limitations of this politico-economic model. The United States and other advanced industrial states are sharply criticizing Japan for pursuing neomercantilist policies and practices that have the effect of exporting the social costs of economic adjustment abroad. Moreover, developmental corporatism has begun to burden the Japanese economy with rigidities (especially in the labor market), inefficiencies (e.g., in the distribution system), and excessive or misguided investments as Japan operates increasingly on the frontiers of technology.

In Japan, the sharpest intellectual critique of developmental corporatism has come from analysts who embrace the "economic liberalism" of Anglo-American neoconservatives. They argue that Japan must deregulate the economy and lift protectionist barriers, scale back the interventionist policies of state bureaucrats, make more transparent to foreign competitors the norms and rules of Japanese business, and incorporate greater flexibility in the labor market by modifying the practice of "permanent employment" (Kato, 1990). On the whole, these Japanese "economic liberals" have supported the efforts of successive U.S. administrations to liberalize the Japanese economy. But because they want to reduce the role of the state in the economy, they adamantly reject the Clinton Administration's results-oriented approach to bilateral trade negotiations. In their view, the adoption of "qualitative and quantitative measures of progress" regarding foreign access to the Japanese market would be interpreted as "numerical targets" and increase the power of Japanese bureaucrats. Although the liberal critique of developmental corporatism is intellectually attractive, it suffers from being unable to overcome the formidable political and institutional obstacles to deregulation. Despite the vigorous calls for economic liberalization from numerous blue-ribbon commissions and political leaders as well as professional economists, actual progress has been extremely limited.

Neoconservative liberalism could get a boost from the big business sector, which is facing severe challenges from yen appreciation. When Akio Morita, then the chairman of Sony Corporation, first wrote in 1993 a series of essays critical of Japanese economic policy and business practices, he garnered little support from the mainstream business community (Morita, February 1993; Morita, June 1993). His colleagues merely embraced the slogan of *kyosei* or harmonization without pressing for a radical altering of Japanese business culture. But more and more business leaders are recognizing that the corrective mechanism of floating exchange rates is not working because Japan's economy is overregulated and overprotected. Powerful business organizations such as the Keizai Doyukai and Keidranren have criticized bureaucrats and politicians for being so lame about pushing deregulation.[3] The head of Nikkeiren has energetically pressed for passing the benefits of yen appreciation onto consumers in the public utilities and transportation sectors. But the ability of the business community to push the policy process toward economic liberalism remains an open question. In many respects, the business sector itself is divided. There are differences in perspective between export-oriented firms, which are suffering from yen appreciation, and import-oriented firms, which are benefiting not only from yen appreciation, but also from their privileged position in existing markets. There are also conflicts between businesses

---

[3]See for example, Keizai Doyu Kai, 1994.

that want to break out of the constraints of state regulation and those that wish to remain under the protective regulatory umbrella. Therefore, these divisions will hamper the business community's ability to become an effective political force behind economic liberalization.

A less articulate, and perhaps less influential, critique of developmental corporatism has come from social democrats and progressive intellectuals (Masamura, 1994). They see Japan's problem as being an excessive preoccupation with developmentalism, and not the corporatist policies and practices to preserve a social consensus. For them, "developmentalism" has meant the sacrifice of consumer and worker interests in order to provide adequate capital and insulated markets for business expansion and innovation. As a consequence, average Japanese citizens have not enjoyed the fruits of national economic success to the fullest extent possible. What Japan must do is not to dismantle the corporatist policies that have protected the more economically vulnerable social sectors, but rather to transform this corporatism into a more mature welfare state. This "social democratic" alternative would involve a significant reduction of annual working hours, increased investments in social capital, more extensive welfare programs, and less emphasis on capital accumulation. This type of economic reform would expand domestic demand and moderate the corporate drive for foreign economic expansion.

Although social democratic policies would effectively correct Japan's trade and current account surpluses and thereby establish a more politically sustainable economic equilibrium with the United States, the social democratic critique of Japanese developmentalism has an even weaker political base than the economic liberal critique. To the extent that social democrats are influential, they serve primarily as restraints on liberal-oriented reforms. On the other hand, economic liberals have had the effect of discrediting social democratic ideas by referring to the economic difficulties now being experienced by the social democratic states of Western Europe. The political effect of this debate between economic liberals and social democrats has been to weaken the voices for economic reform and to help sustain developmental corporatism.

Political immobilism may not be the only reason for the survival of developmental corporatism. Powerful and articulate voices have recently emerged that praise Japanese-style capitalism and criticize the inhumane aspects of economic liberalism as practiced by the United States. For example, Eisuke Sakakibara of the Finance Ministry argues that Japanese policies and business practices place greater priority on worker welfare and security, and therefore prevent the rise of vexing social problems seen in the West. The socialization of economic risk in the Japanese system also encourages innovation and technological development (Sakakibara, 1993). In short, the dogmatic pursuit of market efficiency as in the United States may destroy the social foundations of capitalism. Therefore, even while pursuing deregulation, Japan should maintain the positive features of managed capitalism.

Rise of "New Asianism"

As part of their search for a national identity appropriate for the post–Cold War era, influential intellectuals are increasingly emphasizing Japan's social and cultural affinity with East Asia. This rediscovery of East Asia resonates with the evolution of Japan's economic interests and the growing anxiety about the reduction of U.S. military presence in the Pacific. The "New Asianism," however, has several variants.

One brand of "re-Asianization" seeks a better integration between Japan's America policy and Japan's Asia policy. The purpose of this "integrationist" approach is to revitalize America's presence and interest in East Asia. Proponents of this view believe that Japan's position in East Asia would become highly problematic if the United States were to lose interest in the region. Consequently, the challenge for Japan is to help the United States revitalize its economic presence in East Asia, to support Washington's efforts to promote human rights and democratization in the region, and to shoulder more of the burden for maintaining U.S. military forces in the Pacific (Okazaki, 1993). The integrationists oppose measures that would divide the Pacific between the East Asian and North American spheres. Therefore, they strongly support the concept of an *Asia-Pacific* community, as opposed to an East Asian grouping.

A second version of the new Asianism sees Japan as playing a key role in an "Asian restoration." By being the first East Asian country to become an advanced industrial democracy and the only East Asian member of the G-7 summit process, Japan could play a unique role in bridging the political and cultural gap between East Asian countries and the United States. In terms of politics, Japan could urge the United States to be more sensitive to the dilemma between economic development and political stability while the latter presses East Asian countries on human rights. In this vein, the Japanese could argue that there is an Asian road to democracy that may be more effective in the long run than the precarious path taken by post-Soviet Russia. On the economic front, Japan could articulate the virtues of the so-called "East Asian model of development" based upon state-business cooperation as opposed to the liberal, monetarist approach to development favored by the World Bank and many U.S. policymakers and economists. Like the integrationists, the "restorationists" are committed to the basic principles of liberal democracy and market economics. But they also see a need for the West to learn from Asia. For example, one senior Japanese diplomat who has written extensively about Asian restoration states that "Americans . . . must actively try to understand Asia and learn from it, accepting some Asian values in the process" (Ogura, 1993). And unlike the integrationists who strongly oppose Malaysian Prime Minister Mahathir's proposal for an East Asia Economic Caucus, the restorationists believe that such a grouping could be worthwhile if developed under the broader rubric of the Asia-Pacific.

Finally, there is an "exclusivist" version of re-Asianization that sees an estrangement between Japan and the United States as virtually inevitable and perhaps healthy. Exclusivists argue that Japan should become less dependent upon the United States and ground its foreign policy more in East Asia. This perspective stems primarily from an emotional backlash against the "unreasonable" demands from the United States and does not represent a well-thought-out strategy (Ishihara and Akio, 1989; see also Ishihara and Mahathir, 1994). The basic weakness of this position is that the most vocal proponents of developing a concept of East Asia exclusive of the United States are the most reluctant to acknowledge the suffering Japan imposed on its Asian neighbors during the imperialist period. Consequently, this version of the new Asianism will not win much support in the rest of East Asia and will be as misguided as the 1930s vision of a "Greater East Asian Co-Prosperity Sphere" (see Ienaga, 1978).

Currently, the mainstream debate about the re-Asianization of Japanese foreign policy is between the integrationists and the restorationists. As Japan's economic links with the East Asian countries deepen and as the East Asian countries become more comfortable with Japanese power, the influence of the restorationist perspective will grow relative to that of the integrationists. The ascendancy of exclusivism will occur only if relations between Japan and the United States worsen because of an intensification of bilateral economic conflicts coupled with a weakening of America's security commitment to Japan.

PUBLIC OPINION

Public opinion surveys have revealed the following views among the Japanese populace regarding certain key issues:

- Positive and accommodative views toward the United States remain high. But at the same time, there are clear indications that negative and less accommodative views may rise if bilateral economic relations become more problematic.

- The Japanese public still does not view the countries of East Asia as attractive alternatives to the United States and other Western states for international alignments. Pan-Asian thinking has a long way to go before it captures the imagination of a majority of Japanese.

- The Japanese public strongly supports continuity in security policy, while at the same time becoming more receptive to debating openly the issue of constitutional revision.

Generally Positive Views of the United States

The annual surveys conducted by the Prime Minister's Office (PMO) on foreign affairs show that a large majority of Japanese continue to feel a close relationship with the United States (see Figure 4.1). The recent polls conducted by the *Yomiuri Shimbun*, however, have been less positive. Although the United States still ranks first as the most trustworthy country for the Japanese, there was a sharp drop in the percentage of those surveyed who felt this way from 56 percent in 1991 to 45 percent in 1993 (see Figure 4.2). There are also signs of

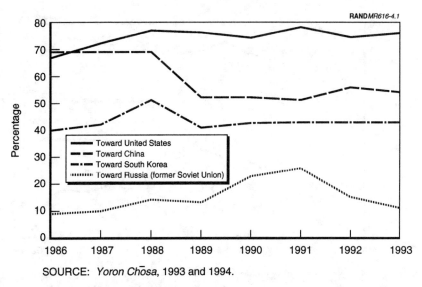

SOURCE: *Yoron Chōsa*, 1993 and 1994.

Figure 4.1—Japanese Public Opinion: Feeling of Affinity Toward the United States, China, South Korea, and Russia

public concern about U.S.-Japan relations. The polling done by *Yomiuri Shimbun* suggests that the positive assessment of bilateral relations has gradually declined over time, while the negative assessment has increased (see Figure 4.3). The PMO surveys give a similar result, although the decline in a positive evaluation of U.S.-Japan relations is not as sharp (see Figure 4.4).

More worrisome are the findings of a survey research project conducted by the Institute of International Relations at Sophia University. Sophia scholars implemented two surveys—one in 1972 and the other in 1992—to collect data on Japanese attitudes toward international society. One question asked which country the respondent felt was the most threatening (see Table 4.1). In 1972, more Japanese saw the Soviet Union (24 percent) as more threatening than any other country. The United States ranked third with 12 percent. In 1992, however, the United States ranked first as the threatening country with 25 percent, just ahead of the former Soviet Union with 24 percent. The Sophia survey also asked about the ap-

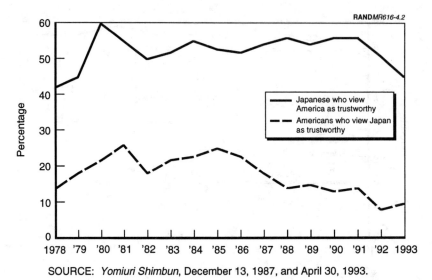

SOURCE: *Yomiuri Shimbun*, December 13, 1987, and April 30, 1993.

Figure 4.2—Japanese Views of America and American Views of Japan

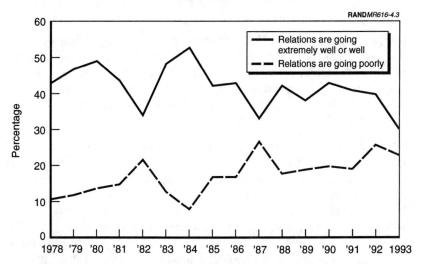

SOURCE: Public opinion surveys conducted annually in the fall
by *Yomiuri Shimbun*.

Figure 4.3—Japanese Public Opinion: State of U.S.-Japan Relations
(*Yomiuri Shimbun* Survey)

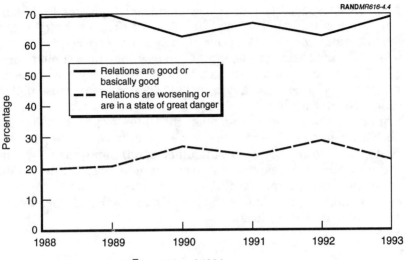

SOURCE: *Yoron Chōsa*, 1993 and 1994.

**Figure 4.4—Japanese Public Opinion: State of U.S.-Japan Relations
(Prime Minister's Office Survey)**

Table 4.1

Japanese Public Opinion: Country That Is Most Threatening

*Question: Among the various countries of the world, which country
do you feel to be most threatening?*

Threatening Country	1972 (%)	Threatening Country	1992 (%)
Soviet Union	24	United States	25
China	13	Former Soviet Union	24
United States	12	China	11
Other Asian countries	1	North Korea	7
Western European		South Korea	
countries	1		3
All countries	3	Germany	2
No country is threatening		No country is threaten-	
or not clear	12	ing or not clear	27

SOURCE: Watanuki, 1993.

propriate approach to Japan-U.S. economic relations (see Table 4.2). The findings were ambiguous. In 1972, 13 percent thought that Japan should accommodate economically to preserve good relations with the United States; while in 1992, 28 percent held a similar opinion. But the results also indicated a significant increase in attitudes that were less accommodative. In 1972, 32 percent of those polled indicated that while maintaining good relations with the United States, Japan need not accommodate the United States economically because Japan has its own perspective. Twenty years later, 42 percent expressed this view. On the other hand, there was a drop in the percentage of respondents who thought that Japan should strengthen its economic ties with other countries without being concerned about good relations with the United States (18 percent in 1972 and 12 percent in 1992).

Table 4.2

Japanese Public Opinion: U.S.-Japan Economic Relations

Question: Regarding relations between Japan and the United States, the American economy is not doing very well and there is now a conflict of economic interests between the two countries. What is your opinion regarding this?

Response	1972 (%)	1992 (%)
In order to maintain good relations with the United States, Japan should accommodate economically.	13	28
While maintaining good relations with the United States, Japan given its own position has no need to accommodate the United States economically.	32	42
Without being concerned about good relations with the United States, Japan should strengthen its economic relations with other countries.	18	12
Other responses.	3	1
Don't know.	34	18
Total (100%)	(2,967)	(1,395)

SOURCE: Watanuki, 1993.

Less Positive Views Toward Ties with Other Asian Countries as Alternatives to the U.S. Relationship

Despite discussions about the re-Asianization of Japanese foreign policy at the elite level, the Japanese public's attitudes toward other countries in East Asia are not as positive as those toward the United States.   In the PMO surveys, the Asian country toward which Japanese have felt the greatest affinity is China, but the gap between the United States and China is about 20 percentage points. During the late 1980s, the PMO surveys indicated that close to 70 percent harbored close feelings toward China (see Figure 4.1).   After the Tiananmen massacre in 1989, this positive view declined sharply to about 50 percent. Since then, there has been a gradual recovery of these favorable views. The *Yomiuri Shimbun* surveys show an even sharper drop in the percentage of Japanese who felt China to be trustworthy after the Tiananmen massacre (see Figure 4.5).

Japanese attitudes toward South Korea tend to be even less positive than those toward China. The PMO surveys show that only about 40

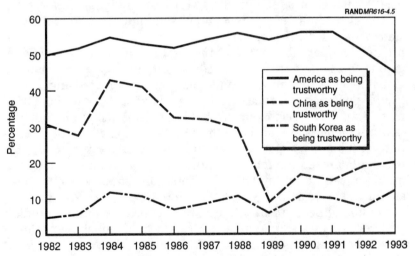

SOURCE: *Yomiuri Shimbun*, December 13, 1987, and April 30, 1993.

Figure 4.5—Japanese Views of America, China, and South Korea

percent of the Japanese have close feelings toward South Korea. As Figure 4.1 shows, Japanese views of Korea have remained relatively constant. The *Yomiuri Shimbun* polls (Figure 4.5) also indicate that fewer Japanese feel South Korea is trustworthy than those who see China as being trustworthy. In 1993, China and South Korea ranked eighth and ninth respectively in terms of trustworthiness after the United States, Britain, Australia, Germany, France, Canada, and Switzerland, in that order (from first to seventh).

Japanese views of Russia and the Soviet Union have been strongly negative. But in the context of Soviet reform, positive feelings toward Russia increased steadily during the late 1980s. In 1991, the percentage of Japanese who felt close to the Soviet Union reached a peak of 25.4 percent in the PMO survey. But these positive views dropped again to 15.2 percent the following year after Russian President Boris Yeltsin canceled his scheduled visit to Japan.

Regarding the issue of economic regionalism, the PMO survey indicates that a plurality of Japanese favor economic cooperation in the Asia-Pacific region simultaneously with economic cooperation at the global level. In a 1993 poll, 43.8 percent supported the following statement: "Because Japan is a member of the Asia-Pacific, it should promote cooperation on the economic front in the Asia-Pacific region at the same time as it promotes economic cooperation at the global level." By contrast, only 19.2 percent favored the strictly globalist perspective articulated by the following: "Not limiting itself to the Asia-Pacific region, Japan should promote economic cooperation from a global perspective through the Uruguay Round." Support for a strictly regionalist position was even weaker. Only 15.4 percent endorsed the following position: "Given the unification of the European Community, Japan should promote economic cooperation in Asia as a priority" (*Yoron Chosa*, 1994, pp. 28–29). In short, the public appears to back the mainstream view among opinion leaders that Japan should pursue a regional and global policy simultaneously and should try to bridge East Asia and the West.

Continuity in Security Policy Coupled with Constitutional Reform

PMO surveys show that a large majority of those polled favor maintenance of the U.S.-Japan security system and Self-Defense Forces as the best way to protect Japan's security (see Figure 4.6). And a majority would like to keep the defense budget at current levels (see Figure 4.7). Since 1978, there has been a steady increase in the percentage of those who would like to reduce the defense budget. In short, little support exists for major rearmament and a move beyond a strictly defensive military doctrine.

While favoring basic continuity in security policy, the public appears to be more receptive to tackling the constitutional revision issue head on. The *Yomiuri Shimbun* polls show a sharp increase after 1991 in the percentage of those supporting revision of the constitution (see Figure 4.8). This change probably reflects a widespread feeling that Japan could not respond effectively to the Persian Gulf crisis of 1990–1991 because of constitutional constraints.

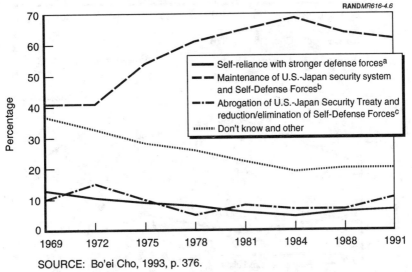

SOURCE: Bo'ei Cho, 1993, p. 376.

[a]Preserve Japan's security by relying solely on the nation's own power—i.e., by abrogating the U.S.-Japan Security Treaty and strengthening the defense forces.

[b]Preserve Japan's security by maintaining the current policy of relying on the U.S.-Japan security system and the Self-Defense Forces.

[c]Abrogate the U.S.-Japan Security Treaty and either reduce or eliminate the Self-Defense Forces.

Figure 4.6—Japanese Public Opinion: Protecting Japan's Security

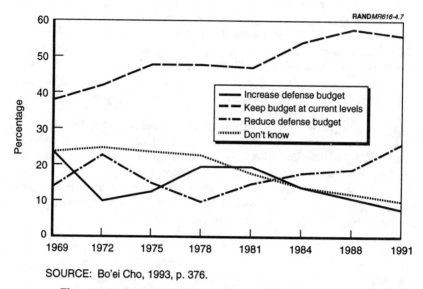

SOURCE: Bo'ei Cho, 1993, p. 376.

Figure 4.7—Japanese Public Opinion: Size of the Defense Budget

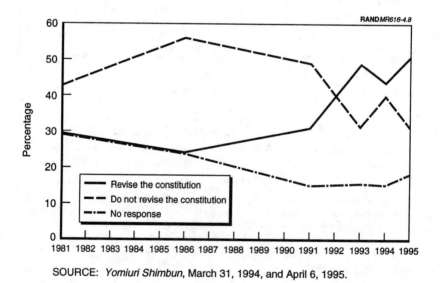

SOURCE: *Yomiuri Shimbun*, March 31, 1994, and April 6, 1995.

Figure 4.8—Public Attitude Toward Constitutional Revision

In the *Yomiuri Shimbun* survey conducted in March 1995, 50.4 percent of the respondents favored revising the constitution compared with 30.9 percent who opposed. Of those who endorsed constitutional revision, the largest percentage (56.9 percent) believed that such a change is necessary because new challenges such as international contribution are emerging that cannot be handled under the current constitution (*Yomiuri Shimbun*, April 6, 1995). Despite this trend toward growing support for constitutional revision, the public remains sharply divided on this issue as corroborated by a study conducted by Sophia University (see Table 4.3).

GENERATIONAL CHANGE

At both the elite and popular levels, generational change can be a powerful driver of attitudinal change. Numerous analysts have argued that Japan's economic success has made the younger generation much more self-confident. In contrast to the older generation that experienced as adults the tragedy of misguided militarism, defeat, and reconstruction, the postwar generation tends to see the world from the vantage point of Japan as an economic superpower. In some instances, this self-confidence can manifest itself as a sense

Table 4.3

Japanese Public Opinion: Issue of Constitutional Revision

Question: What do you think about the current constitution?

	1972	1992
Because the current constitution goes too far on many points, it should be revised as soon as possible to better reflect the national situation of Japan.	22	31
Because the current constitution is on the whole a fine document, it should not be revised for the time being.	36	40
Can't say either way.	18	17
Don't know.	25	12
Total	2,967	1,395

SOURCE: Public opinion surveys conducted by the Institute of International Relations at Sophia University in May–June 1972 and December 1992.

of Japanese superiority over the West. In other cases, this attitude will accentuate the relative decline of the United States (Pyle, 1992, p. 50). Although it is far from clear how this generational shift will shape foreign policy, the probability is high that Japanese will be less deferential and accommodative toward American demands than before. Prime Minister Hosokawa's saying "no" to President Bill Clinton's effort to urge Japan to adopt import targets won widespread praise throughout the media world and the public at large. But in more positive terms, economic success may also encourage the new generation of Japanese leaders to interpret their national interests in broader terms. Rather than considering international issues narrowly for their impact on the domestic economy, younger leaders may become more prone to take a proactive attitude toward external problems (Lincoln, 1993, pp. 51–55).

At the public level, opinion polls suggest a moderate increase in nationalistic sentiments. For example, the surveys conducted by NHK (the Japan Broadcasting Corporation) every five years indicate such a trend. In 1973, 41 percent of the respondents felt that Japan was a "first-class country" (*ichiryu koku*). Ten years later in 1983, 57 percent had such an assessment of their country. This percentage declined to 50 percent in 1988 (NHK Yoron Chosabu, 1991, p. 101). A similar trend is discernible regarding the issue of internationalization. According to a PMO survey in 1987, 40.8 percent supported internationalization as an international obligation incurred by Japan for becoming a major power (*taikoku*). Those holding this view increased to 48.2 percent in 1991, followed by a drop to 45.7 percent in 1993. There are, however, clear gender differences regarding internationalization. In the 1993 survey, while 53.4 percent of men surveyed saw internationalization as an obligation of a major power, only 39.0 percent of the women held this view. Generational differences were much greater among women than among men. For men, 54.6 percent between the ages of 20–49 considered internationalization as an obligation compared with 52.4 percent of the 50 and above age cohort. In the case of women, 44.3 percent in the younger group supported this view compared with only 32.2 percent in the older group (*Yoron Chosa*, April 1994, pp. 3–4).

Beyond the emergence of a new nationalism and even a new internationalism, generational change can also alter the social dynamics within Japan, which in turn could have international consequences.

Brought up under affluence, younger Japanese appear to be less committed to long work hours and loyalty to one's corporate organization. Instead of seeing the workplace as the center of one's existence and the source of one's lifetime satisfaction, the postwar generation (especially those born in the 1960s and 1970s) are more interested in leisure and consumption. The emergence of this new class of "pleasure seekers," many of whom are children of wealthy and propertied families, may not only weaken the social norm of diligence and frugality, but also undermine Japan's egalitarian and meritocratic society (Emmott, 1989, pp. 25–74). All of this suggests that there may be social limits to Japan's economic juggernaut. Japan could follow a path similar to the advanced industrial societies of the West, where work discipline has become more problematic. As Japan transforms itself from a nation of savers to a nation of consumers, it will cease to be the neomercantilist state that poses an economic challenge to the United States.

Recent surveys offer some empirical evidence for this shift in Japanese attitudes toward work. In its quinquennial surveys, NHK has asked whether they place greater priority on work, on leisure, or on work and leisure equally. Over the years, there has been a clear decline in the percentage of those who put greater priority on work over leisure. In 1973, 44 percent were work-oriented; but in 1988, only 31 percent were so inclined. Those who favored giving work and leisure equal importance increased from 21 percent in 1973 to 32 percent in 1988. But the percentage of those who are leisure-oriented has held steady: 32 percent in 1973 and 34 percent in 1988. If one analyzes the data in generational terms, those born in later years have a greater tendency to support the notion of balancing work and leisure rather than emphasizing only work (NHK Yoron Chosabu, 1991, pp. 67–69).

One, however, has to be cautious in assessing the impact of generational change. Social behavior and norms evident during youth may not stick as an age cohort grows older. The attitudinal differences across generations could express more life-cycle differences than generational ones. People in their youth are likely to be more carefree and rebellious. But as they take on family and job responsibilities, such tendencies will subside. The rebellious youth of the late 1950s and late 1960s have become the hardworking, loyal executives and employees of today. Similarly the so-called "new breed"

(*shinjinrui*) of today could go through a similar evolution. The socialization mechanisms of Japanese schools, corporations, and families remain powerful. In many ways, the new breed phenomenon
may have been just a manifestation of the 1980s bubble economy.
The prolonged recession of the early 1990s along with such traumatic
events as the great Hanshin earthquake and the sarin gas attack
could reinforce the Japanese sense of vulnerability and revitalize
traditional norms in favor of diligence and group loyalty.

Chapter Five

IMPLICATIONS FOR JAPANESE FOREIGN POLICY AND EXTERNAL BEHAVIOR

BASIC PARAMETERS OF JAPANESE FOREIGN POLICY AND EXTERNAL BEHAVIOR

Given the fluid domestic situation in Japan today, it is impossible to predict with precision the actual policies that Japan will pursue during the next decade. Much will depend upon the concrete choices made by Japanese leaders at critical moments in the transition process. But the outcomes that are likely to emerge will certainly fall within some clear parameters. These parameters include

- Maintenance of the security relationship with the United States in some form.

- Promotion of multilateral security fora in the Asia-Pacific region as a complement, not a replacement, to the U.S.-Japan security relationship. This would be connected with greater Japanese interest in confidence and security-building measures.

- Increasing Japanese participation in the United Nations—in the security realm, as well as the humanitarian, economic, and cultural realms.

- Closer integration with East Asian economies through trade, investments, and technology flows and support of the Asia-Pacific Economic Cooperation (APEC) process. This would be not only for economic reasons. Japan will also try to use increasing regional economic interdependence as a way of mitigating security uncertainties.

But within these parameters, there will be room for substantial variations.

POLITICAL-MILITARY DIMENSION

There are two key questions regarding the political-military dimension of Japanese foreign policy. First, will Japan emerge as a more "normal" country, whereby it wields political-military influence more commensurate with its economic power, or will Japan remain as what some have called a "moratorium state"—a state that is passive and reactive diplomatically and minimalist in terms of defense policy (Nagai, 1981)? Second, if Japan were to become more proactive in the political-military arena, how is Japan likely to pursue this activism?

Up to now, two factors kept Japan as a "moratorium state." One was the U.S. security umbrella, which gave Japan the luxury of avoiding difficult diplomatic choices and keeping its military expenditures low. To the extent that Japan had a security policy, it was to calibrate what was necessary to sustain America's security commitment to Japan. The other factor was the domestic political stalemate between two ideologically divergent conceptions of national security: realism in alliance with the United States and pacifistic neutralism. This stalemate made it difficult at times to respond decisively on behalf of U.S. expectations about Japanese burden-sharing in the security realm. Japan's tortured response to the Persian Gulf crisis of 1990–1991 is a good example of this.

However, the end of the Cold War and the problem of North Korea's nuclear program in the context of domestic political realignment could steer Japan away from its moratorium status.

Review of the National Defense Program Outline

A key benchmark for the future of Japanese defense policy will be the revision of the National Defense Program Outline (NDPO), which has guided defense procurements since 1976. Because the NDPO was drafted during the height of Soviet-American détente, a number of civilian security policy specialists as well as SDF officers supported revising the 1976 outline in response to the increasing Soviet military threat at both the regional and global levels during the late 1970s and 1980s. But given the strong commitment of the Japan Defense Agency (JDA) to the "Outline" as well as opposition from dovish politicians, the NDPO continued to serve as the primary guide for national defense policy throughout the 1980s. With the end of the Cold War, however, JDA officials came to recognize the necessity of NDPO revision. And with the decline of the SDPJ's electoral power as well as political realignment, they saw an opportunity to depolarize the politics of security policy once and for all.

In taking the lead in drafting a new policy outline, the JDA has adopted the following approach: Consult widely, develop a strong national consensus behind the country's defense policies, and minimize political controversy. Accordingly, the agency will refrain from pushing initiatives that may go far beyond the majority public opinion. This means that the agency will support maintaining a strictly defensive military posture and will only gingerly promote the idea of deepening military cooperation with the United States for regional security beyond defense of the home islands. It also means that the NDPO revision process will reconfirm Japan's nonnuclear policy despite concerns about North Korean nuclear proliferation. While taking the lead, the JDA has been consulting with other bureaucratic agencies (e.g., the Ministries of Foreign Affairs, Finance, and International Trade and Industry) with a keen interest in security.

Although work on NDPO revision is in progress, JDA officials are considering the following subjects for inclusion in the new outline (Defense Agency Officials, 1993):

- An assessment of medium- and long-term geopolitical and economic trends, including the probable reunification of Korea, the inevitable rise of Chinese power, the emergence of regional tensions because of demographic pressures and competition for energy sources and markets, and the need to maintain U.S. security presence in the region.

- Promotion of military consultations and joint planning and exercises with the United States to deal with regional security contingencies.

- Improvement in the institutional and legal framework for dealing with national and international security issues.

- The need to buttress the network of bilateral security relationships between the United States and the various Pacific countries with multilateral security consultations, and the inadequacy of U.N.-centered approaches to deal with the changing Asia-Pacific security environment.

- A reduction in the size of authorized forces—especially ground forces—to reduce costs and develop a more efficient defense posture.

- Strengthening Japan's ability to participate in U.N. peacekeeping activities.

While deliberations about the details of the new NDPO have so far taken place primarily within and across bureaucratic agencies and away from public view, discussions will become increasingly public and subject to political intervention as the review process proceeds. In February 1994, then Prime Minister Hosokawa appointed an advisory panel called the Bo'ei Mondai Kondankai (Defense Issues Discussion Group or DIDG) headed by Hirotaro Higuchi (chairman of Asahi Breweries) to make recommendations regarding a new defense policy outline.[1] Both his successors to the prime ministership, Tsutomu Hata and Tomiichi Murayama, have endorsed the NDPO review process and the work of the Higuchi panel. Since this commission represents mainstream thinking on defense issues and has incorporated many of the ideas of JDA officials, its August 1994 report is likely to be the basis for defense planning well into the 21st century, barring radical changes in the international environment. This document therefore demands careful scrutiny.

---

[1]The other members of this advisory panel are Ken Moroi (chairman of Chichibu Cement), Kuniko Inoguchi (professor at Sophia University), Yoshio Okawara (special advisor to Keidanren), Yukio Gyoten (chairman of the Bank of Tokyo), Hajime Sakuma (special counselor to Nippon Telegraph and Telephone Company), Seiki Nishihiro (advisor to Tokyo Marine and Fire), Shinji Fukukawa (vice-chairman of Kobe Steel), and Akio Watanabe (professor at Aoyama Gakuin University). Initially, the JDA appears to have resented this move because of concerns about the limited participation of security policy experts and possible outside interference in their own review process. And given the relatively "dovish" composition of the Higuchi panel, Defense Minister Kazuo Aichi (a leader of the prodefense Shinseito) formed his own defense study group to advise the Hosokawa Cabinet.

Even while arguing that Japan must play a more proactive role in developing a stable international order and shift from a "Cold War defense strategy" to a "multilateral security strategy," the DIDG proposed only moderate changes from the policies enunciated in the 1976 NDPO.[2] As in the NDPO, the commission emphasized how the security relationship with the United States and the credibility of American extended nuclear deterrence are critical to Japanese security. It noted the direct link between a long-term peace strategy of nuclear disarmament and the objective of strengthening U.S.-Japan security cooperation. Many of the DIDG's recommendations mirrored those found in the NDPO: (1) strengthening bilateral policy consultations and information exchanges; (2) promoting cooperation at the operational level through joint planning, research, and training; (3) establishing a mutual cooperation system for rear support; and (4) furthering mutual cooperation regarding equipment, especially in the area of command, control, communications and intelligence (C^3I).

Two proposals, however, go beyond the 1976 policy guidelines. One concerns a reform of the host-nation support system for U.S. forces in Japan to enhance flexibility in the use of funds and to encourage more joint U.S.-Japan utilization of American base facilities in Japan. The other is a proposal to sign as soon as possible an Acquisition and Cross-Servicing Agreement (ACSA) with the United States similar to that between the United States and its North Atlantic Treaty Organization (NATO) allies regarding mutual assistance for rear support, supplies, and logistical service. The intention here is to permit Japan to provide supplies (including fuel) and transportation for joint U.S.-Japan military exercises (*Yomiuri Shimbun*, July 25, 1994). Both recommendations suggest that the Japanese are interested in making the security relationship more mutual.

In terms of actual defense capabilities, the DIDG affirmed the continuing validity of the so-called "standard defense force" (kibanteki bo'ei ryoku) concept articulated in the 1976 NDPO. According to this concept, Japan needs to maintain the basic and minimal force neces-

---

[2]Presented to Prime Minister Murayama on August 12, 1994, the report was entitled *Nihon no anzen hosho to bo'ei ryoku no arikata: 21 seiki e mukete no tenbo* (DIDG, 1994).

sary to deter small-scale attacks and to repel such an attack, if it were occur, with the help of U.S. forces. Since no threat is likely to emerge in the foreseeable future that could challenge the United States politically and militarily, the Higuchi report stressed the need to prepare for unpredictable dangers, including disturbances to maritime safety, violation of national air space, limited missile attacks, illegal occupation of territory, various terrorist acts, and the entry of armed refugees.

While viewing the "standard defense force" concept as still valid, however, the commission saw the need to restructure the defense forces somewhat. To develop a more effective and efficient defense capability that could respond to unforeseen threats, the DIDG emphasized three considerations: (1) revolutionary changes in military technology, especially in the area of C^3I, which will require longer-range planning for system development and procurement; (2) long-term reduction in the population of young people, which will make SDF recruitment more difficult; and (3) severe budgetary constraints, which will force defense cuts in some areas and greater efficiency in others.

Taking into account these factors, the group outlined several concrete reform measures. At the top of the list was improving the C^3I system, including the use of reconnaissance satellites. Next came greater operational integration among the three services (ground, maritime, and air self-defense forces) to improve efficiency and facilitate effective responses to dangerous developments in the international situation. This would mean that the Joint Chiefs of Staff and their chairman would require greater ability to coordinate operations. It would also mean that at the operational level, force mobility and rapid response capabilities would have to be improved. In considering demographic and budgetary constraints, the DIDG recommended that the overall size of the Self-Defense Force be reduced from the current level of about 274,000 to about 240,000. To compensate in part for this 12.4 percent personnel cutback, the commission recommended consideration of a reserve defense force system.

At the level of the individual services, the DIDG proposed the following changes. For the ground forces, the Higuchi panel emphasized the need to make the various units more flexible and adaptable to a variety of tasks ranging from U.N. peacekeeping activities to domestic disaster relief and rescue operations. It also recommended in the context of personnel reductions that the ground forces shift away from an emphasis on tanks and heavy artillery to a stress on mobility and high-tech weaponry. Regarding maritime forces, the commission called for reductions in ships and planes geared for antisubmarine warfare and antimine operations. Future priority should be on survey and monitoring functions, military engagements against surface ships, and air defense capabilities. Concerning the air forces, the DIDG highlighted the importance of making more efficient and advanced the air warning and control system, including radar sites. It also raised the possibility of acquiring an airborne refueling capability. But given the improbability of air attacks after the Soviet collapse, the number of fighter aircraft and fighter squadrons should be reduced. Finally, to counter threats from ballistic missiles, especially those with nuclear or biochemical warheads, Japan will need to acquire its own ballistic missile defense capabilities.

The greatest change in the DIDG report from the NDPO concerned Japan's contribution to multilateral and cooperative security, in particular participation in U.N. peacekeeping activities. The commission recommended a revision of the Self-Defense Force law to mandate peacekeeping activities as one of the Self-Defense Force's primary duties. In calling for the development of a peacekeeping training center, the group explicitly opposed proposals raised by various pacifist groups for creating a new organization separate from the SDF for peacekeeping operations. Moreover, the DIDG recommended lifting the freeze on SDF participation in U.N. peacekeeping forces (PKF) that was included in the original International Peace Cooperation law passed in 1992.[3] Lifting the PKF freeze would enable the SDF to participate in ceasefire monitoring and other activities that may require light arms.[4] Currently, the SDF's role is limited to transportation, communication, construction, humanitarian relief, election monitoring, and advice on administrative and policy

---

[3] For an analysis of the legislative process leading up to this 1992 law, see Saito, 1992.

[4] These PKF activities include monitoring compliance with cease-fire arrangements; supervising the disarming, withdrawal, or redeployment of troops; patrolling in a buffer zone; checking the movement of weapons; collecting, maintaining, or disposing of discarded weapons; assisting in cease-fire line demarcation; assisting in the exchange of prisoners of war. See Saito, 1992, p. 20.

activities. The DIDG report also highlighted the implications of peacekeeping for defense procurements. The maritime force will have to strengthen its sea transport capabilities and its ability to provide logistical support at sea; and the air force may need to acquire long-range air transport capabilities. In addition to U.N. peacekeeping activities, the DIDG also underscored other ways to promote multilateral security cooperation: official development assistance (ODA), contributions by nongovernmental organizations (NGOs) to security, global regimes to prevent the proliferation of weapons of mass destruction, implementation of the U.N. registry for conventional arms transfer, the promotion of regional institutions for cooperative security like the Association of Southeast Asian Nations (ASEAN) Regional Forum, and various bilateral military exchanges.

Since the main purpose of the DIDG was to cultivate a public consensus for a more proactive security policy, few of its concrete recommendations are likely to provoke political controversy. The most problematic will be the measures regarding participation in U.N. peacekeeping forces. But even here, the recent shift in SDPJ policies will facilitate National Diet approval for such activities. One controversial point may be the acquisition of long-range sea and air transport capabilities. Even though such procurements make sense from the perspective of sending SDF units overseas, they carry the potential of giving Japan a modest force projection capability beyond the official limit of 1,000 nautical miles. The acquisition of airborne refueling tankers would raise similar concerns. On the one hand, social democrats and pacifists are likely to oppose such equipment because they might weaken Japan's commitment to a strictly defensive military doctrine. On the other hand, dovish leaders and groups will welcome the DIDG proposals to downsize the military and to promote cooperative security.

Others will criticize the Higuchi panel for not going far enough. The DIDG report did not make the kind of conceptual breakthrough that many defense analysts have been advocating for some time. While calling for a more proactive and constructive security policy, it did not mention Japan's right to "collective self-defense." Nor did it discuss the concept of "collective security" except in the context of a U.N.-centered collective security system, something that the commission acknowledged would not be realized in the foreseeable future. The DIDG also refrained from considering Japanese participation in multinational peacemaking or peace enforcement operations that are endorsed by the United Nations, but would be executed by a multinational (and not a U.N. blue-helmeted force) as in the Persian Gulf war of 1991. Moreover, while emphasizing the need to improve the nation's crisis management system, the commission did not raise the possibility of playing a broader regional security role in military terms. It also avoided the questions of constitutional reinterpretation or revision and of permanent membership on the U.N. Security Council.

In short, the DIDG's report is essentially a conservative document affirming Japan's commitment to a strictly defensive military posture and a security alliance with the United States. To the extent that there is to be an expansion of Japan's security role, it should take place within the framework of U.N. peacekeeping operations, through the development of multilateral security institutions, and by primarily nonmilitary means. In the final analysis, the document therefore resonates more with the civilian power vision of Japan, than the normal country vision. The degree to which normal country advocates can push their agenda beyond the directions outlined by the DIDG will depend on whether Ozawa and his colleagues in the Shinshinto can win the support of prodefense advocates in the LDP. The current political alignment divides those who desire a more expansive Japanese defense role and a reinterpretation or revision of the constitution into opposing camps. This has the effect of strengthening the hand of civilian power proponents and reinforcing the JDA interest in pushing only incremental changes. All of this would change, however, if Japan's strategic environment were to change dramatically. The most immediate possibility of such a transformation would come as a result of developments on the Korean peninsula.

North Korean Nuclear Issue

During the spring of 1994, Ozawa pushed hard to relax existing policy constraints so that Japan could respond more flexibly to what appeared at the time as an imminent crisis over North Korea's nuclear program. To prevent Japanese paralysis if U.N. endorsement of sanctions against North Korea were not forthcoming because of a

Chinese veto, Ozawa pressed his coalition partners to view the matter in terms of cooperation with the United States and South Korea. He also advocated putting together legislation regarding measures for coping with emergencies and making a conceptual breakthrough in support of collective self-defense. At the same time, he wanted to use the North Korean issue to trigger another political realignment by causing a split within both the LDP and SDPJ. Although this political maneuver ultimately failed and the coalition headed by Tsutomu Hata fell from power, the episode illustrated how international developments can shape domestic politics. If the October 1994 Agreed Framework between Washington and Pyongyang mandating a North Korean freeze of its nuclear program in exchange for light-water reactors collapses, another potential Korean crisis could encourage normal country advocates to put aside personal animosities and coalesce. Such a development could move Japanese military policy beyond the parameters outlined by the DIDG.

How has the North Korean nuclear problem affected Japan's military planning? The only concrete effect thus far has been to accelerate the procurement of a new generation Patriot missile system and to consider the U.S. overture regarding research on a more sophisticated theater missile defense (TMD) system. The predominant view in the JDA has been that the North Korean problem is primarily a short-term issue that requires care and patience, but not something that should decisively mold long-term military planning. But during the tense period in the spring of 1994, both the JDA and the Self-Defense Forces seriously examined the possibility that the United States might ask Japan for rear support in implementing a naval blockade *(Yomiuri Shimbun,* June 8, 1994). Some military analysts even considered how Japan might respond if a war did break out. For example, Hisahiko Okazaki (a former Japanese ambassador to Thailand and Saudi Arabia) saw the possibility that Japanese F-15s might have to enter the conflict to help the United States and South Korea secure air control (Okazaki and Izumi, 1994, p. 102).

What about concerns raised in the United States and elsewhere that Japan itself might go nuclear in response to North Korean nuclearization? Then Foreign Minister Kabun Muto's hesitation in July 1993 to endorse indefinite extension of the Nuclear Non-Proliferation Treaty certainly fueled these suspicions (Schlesinger, 1993). And there have been reports that some Japanese diplomats have privately expressed the need for Japan to keep the nuclear option open *(Asahi Shimbun, November 29, 1992)*. More recently, former Defense Minister Taku Yamazaki stated on national television that he would oppose extending the nonproliferation treaty indefinitely if North Korea is permitted to develop nuclear weapons: "It is necessary for Japan to have a bargaining chip" (NHK Television, 1994). But despite these statements, there is still a robust consensus that Japan should not develop nuclear weapons in response to a North Korean nuclear threat. The so-called "nuclear allergy" among the general public remains in force. Mainstream realist analysts argue that as long as the U.S.-Japan security relationship remains strong and U.S. extended deterrence credible, there is no need to go nuclear. If U.S. extended deterrence has been credible against a much larger and dangerous Soviet and Chinese nuclear threat, why wouldn't it be credible against North Korea? In response to arguments that North Korea is an abnormal, terrorist state very different from either the Soviet Union or China, realists stress that if that were the case, Japanese nuclear acquisition would not be effective as a deterrent anyway. Under such circumstances, the best way to counter a limited North Korean nuclear arsenal would be thorough defensive measures like a TMD system. Therefore, most mainstream strategists strongly advocate Japanese cooperation with the United States in developing a more effective TMD system (Okazaki and Izumi, 1994, p. 105; Yamashita, Susumu, and Shuichiro, 1994, pp. 86–87). Some military analysts in the realist tradition, however, are skeptical about a TMD system's ability to protect Japan from ballistic missiles with nuclear warheads. But even they stop short of backing the acquisition of nuclear weapons for deterrence purposes (Ebata, 1994, pp. 267–278). Pacifists and critics of *realpolitik* approaches, of course, remain committed to a strict nonnuclear policy and endorse the promotion of regional nuclear-free zones as a way of achieving a nonnuclear Korea (Kamo, 1993, pp. 201–202; Yamamoto, 1993). Even romantic nationalists like Shintaro Ishihara do not support Japanese nuclearization (Ishihara, 1990). In short, to the extent that America's security commitment continues to be credible, North Korean acquisition of nuclear weapons capable of attacking Japan is unlikely to compel Japan to engage in a nuclear weapons program of its own.

A reunited Korea with a nuclear arsenal, however, is likely to exert greater pressure on Japan to change its nonnuclear policy than a nuclear North Korea. Such a scenario becomes possible if, in the context of a reunification process prompted by a collapse of the Pyongyang regime, the Republic of Korea decides to maintain and further develop the nuclear facilities of North Korea. The reason why such a development would be particularly alarming to Tokyo is that it would structurally change the security environment in Northeast Asia. First of all, Korean reunification is likely to prompt a reassessment of U.S. military posture in the region. For domestic political reasons, Washington will be hard-pressed to justify a U.S. military presence in Korea after reunification. There may even be pressures to reduce U.S. forces in Japan substantially below levels outlined in a Department of Defense publication. As a consequence, the security link between Washington and Tokyo could weaken. Second, a re-unified Korea may be tempted to maximize its diplomatic leverage by pursuing a foreign policy independent of the major regional powers (Japan, China, Russia, and the United States). The withdrawal of U.S. forces from Korea would give Seoul the freedom to pursue such a strategy. One retired senior Japanese military officer even went so far as to say that after reunification, Korea will lean toward China and/or Russia to counter Japan.[5] Such an alignment would be even more ominous for Japan. Third, given the longstanding cultural and historical distrust (if not outright hostility) between Korea and Japan, the Japanese are likely to see a Korean nuclear arsenal as being targeted against them. And this Korean nuclear threat would emerge at a time when American security ties to Northeast Asia will have weakened. Finally, a reunited Korea will have much greater technological and industrial capabilities than North Korea to develop a potent nuclear arsenal as well as a conventional force capable of threatening Japan. With this combination of factors, it is not hard to imagine a dramatic weakening of Japan's "allergy" to nuclear weapons as well as a dissipation of post–World War II pacifism.

Possible Emergence of Great Power Nationalism

In the final analysis, Japan as either a civilian power or a normal country would be acceptable to U.S. strategic interests. Both alter-

---

[5] Personal interview with a retired Japanese general (Ground Self-Defense Force, 1993).

natives emphasize the primacy of the alliance with the United States. They differ only in terms of the appropriate modality for bilateral security cooperation. But what would be detrimental would be the ascendancy of great power nationalism, whereby Japan develops power projection capabilities and pursues a security policy independent of the United States. Three scenarios could lead to the emergence of this alternative.

The first would involve security abandonment by the United States—because of tensions in economic relations—in the context of increasing Chinese power and the emergence of a hostile Korea after reunification. Nationalistic opinion leaders will then press their case for a more assertive military policy (including the acquisition of nuclear weapons), while pacifistic attitudes wane among the general public.

A second scenario involves the rise of a nationalistic political party. Although the realignment process could initially reinforce moderation in the security policy debate, it could also lay the foundations for repolarization. Under conservative one-party rule, the Liberal Democrats effectively subsumed conservative nationalism, and the ultranationalist right was relegated either to the seamy world of the criminal underground or to the political fringe. To the extent that these elements were interested in foreign policy, they directed their animosity toward the communist states of the former Soviet Union and China. In the current context, further fragmentation of the conservative forces could yield a stridently nationalistic force that would compete for support in the mainstream of electoral politics. With the decline of communism and chronic frictions in U.S.-Japan economic relations, such a force could direct its hostility toward the United States. Moreover, as in Europe, the influx of foreign workers and the social consequences of economic restructuring could strengthen such a nationalistic movement.

Finally, great power nationalism could emerge as a result of a prolonged period of political fluidity and weak governments. Japan would then have great difficulty making decisive and hard choices to deal effectively with the changing international environment. Under these circumstances, Japanese citizens may increasingly feel that their country is being buffeted by hostile external forces. Voices for a more assertive and independent foreign policy backed by a stronger military could become stronger.

FOREIGN ECONOMIC DIMENSION

During the Cold War era when Japan was still trying to reconstruct its economy and catch up with the West, the United States was Japan's most important economic partner—both as an export market and a source of advanced technologies. While Japan will continue to see good economic relations with the United States as critical to its long-term interests in the coming decade, the weight of the United States in Japan's economic calculations is likely to decline relative to East Asia as a whole. Of course, this does not mean that Japan's economic perspective will be narrowly regional. Its economy is far too large and dynamic to be contained in an East Asian sphere. The United States remains Japan's single largest trading partner and a critical source of scientific knowledge and new technologies. As Europe moved toward a unified market, the Japanese invested briskly in various West European countries to strengthen access to that market. And of course, the Middle East continues to be a vital source of petroleum. Japan's economic horizons are indeed global, not regional. Nevertheless, as it looks at its global economic portfolio, Japan's greatest interest during the coming decade will be in East Asia, in particular Southeast Asia and China. From the Japanese perspective, East Asia represents the greatest potential for economic growth—both in terms of exports and returns on investments. Trade and investment figures show only the beginning of this long-term trend. By utilizing the skills and discipline of East Asian workers, Japan can sustain its access to markets outside of the region. Moreover, Japan will be able to use its economic linkages with East Asia to create a more hospitable security environment and to cope with the geopolitical uncertainties of the post–Cold War world. What then are the implications of this trend for Japan's foreign economic policies?

Economic Relations with the United States

Over the years, Washington has pursued a combination of policies to improve American access to the Japanese market and to alleviate the disruptive effect of increasing imports from Japan: exchange rate adjustments, market-opening measures for specific sectors, restraints on Japanese exports, and pressures to deregulate and stimulate the Japanese economy. During every round of bilateral negotiations, Japanese officials have stubbornly resisted American requests and demands at least initially, only to accommodate later on various points to avoid U.S. economic sanctions. Influential Japanese politicians often intervened in a timely manner to work out a compromise and to avert a crisis in bilateral relations. These have worked to improve U.S. market access at least at the margins. U.S. exports to Japan have increased significantly, and the trade deficit with Japan has declined somewhat in yen terms. Nevertheless, Japan continues to have a large trade and current account surplus with the United States.

At the macroeconomic level, the bilateral imbalances represent the basic asymmetry between a Japan with a high savings rate and a United States with a high consumption rate. To increase Japanese consumption, the government would have to spend more and to change the tax structure to encourage consumption over savings; and firms would have to allocate more of their profits to their workers and less to investments in productive capacity. But for the foreseeable future, Japan is unlikely to follow this path. While supporting short-term fiscal stimulus packages, the MOF wants to avoid chronic deficit financing and is preoccupied with ballooning costs of social welfare programs as the Japanese population ages. Moreover, rather than supporting a long-term reduction in taxes to put more money in the hands of consumers, the ministry stubbornly supports a hike in the consumption tax to offset a cut in income taxes. Except for some debates about the timing of tax reform, almost all of the leading political parties share the fiscal conservatism of the MOF. Therefore, even after elections under the new system, no political force is likely to emerge to overpower the MOF on fiscal affairs. In terms of the business sector, after investing wildly in productive capacity and dubious real estate holdings, many of the major firms now prefer to use their accumulated wealth for restructuring and not for wage increases—especially at a time when they are being forced to implement employee "rationalization" programs and scale back on new hires. In short, Japan's savings rate will remain an order of magnitude higher than that of the United States—at least until Japan's demographic profile is skewed more toward the elderly who theoretically will consume their savings. But this will not happen until after the year 2010.

At the microeconomic level, Japan will gradually implement a variety of deregulation measures, particularly in the distribution sector. This will loosen somewhat the barriers to new business entrants, and encourage price competition. For the consumer sector, the differential between domestic and foreign prices will diminish, making foreign products more attractive to Japanese consumers. But this will not necessarily mean that U.S. producers will be able to sell more in Japan. It is quite possible that inexpensive, yet high-quality, products made in East Asian countries—often through Japanese investments or subsidiaries—will be more attractive in a deregulated Japanese market than American products. Much will hinge on the ability and willingness of U.S. firms to invest in Japan to tap accurately Japanese consumer preferences and to engage in effective designing and marketing. Unfortunately, the high value of the yen makes such American investments extremely costly. As for business purchases of intermediate goods, equipment and parts, the preferential trading practices of Japanese firms for their fellow *keiretsu* members will continue to place foreign producers at a distinct disadvantage. Of course, yen appreciation will force many firms to look for American suppliers in some instances. But at the same time, the pressures of restructuring during a recession will give firms an incentive to socialize the costs of restructuring among *keiretsu* firms by tolerating relatively high-cost purchases from Japanese suppliers and forgoing lower-cost foreign suppliers.

These structural factors will prevent a quick and easy solution to the bilateral trade imbalance. From the perspective of U.S. strategic interests, the key question is how responsive will Japanese policymakers be to strong-armed American trade tactics. As Japan clumsily searches for a new party system, elected governments may be too weak or too preoccupied domestically to accommodate U.S. pressures in a timely manner. Moreover, politicians may feel that there may be some political rewards to be gained for standing up to the Americans and saying "no." If Washington then chooses to implement sanctions as reprisal for Tokyo's uncooperative behavior, Tokyo is likely to use the World Trade Organization as a multilateral dispute resolution mechanism, rather than to escalate the conflict by engaging in countersanctions. Japanese leaders will become more disposed to reject U.S. trade demands as Japan's economic penetration into East Asian countries advances. Insofar as these countries rely heavily on Japanese aid, capital, and even technology, they are likely to be sympathetic to Tokyo's viewpoint in its struggles with Washington. Moreover, given that many of these countries see Japan as an economic model to be emulated, they may support Japan against the United States for fear that Washington may eventually make the same demands on them as it does on Tokyo.

Asia-Pacific Regionalism and Economic Integration with East Asia

Despite its growing economic presence in East Asia, Japan wants to avoid a division in the Asia-Pacific region between NAFTA members and East Asian economies or between the Anglo-American and East Asian states. And Japan would like to avoid a choice between Asia and the West. Given that the United States is still the chief absorber of excess East Asian production, the Japanese recognize that a self-contained East Asian economic bloc is not feasible. For Japan to play such an absorber role for a region engaged in export-led development, it would have to absorb enormous socioeconomic adjustment costs. China has the potential to become a large reserve market for an East Asian economic system, but that country too is engaged in export-led growth and has sizeable trade surpluses with both the United States and Japan. Moreover, most Japanese recognize that an economic dividing line down the Pacific is likely to weaken America's security commitment to its East Asian allies. Therefore, at least in terms of policy rhetoric, Tokyo will vigorously promote the cause of "Asia-Pacific," rather than East Asian economic cooperation. At the same time, reflecting its global economic interests, Japan will strongly endorse the notion of "constructive and open regionalism." This concept refers to the use of regionalism as an instrument "to bring about free and non-discriminatory trade and investment on a global scale." Accordingly, the discriminatory and exclusive features of regional economic blocs would be minimized, while the trade and investment liberalization features would be maximized (Kobayashi, Nakamura, Ito, and Watanabe, 1994, pp. 13–18). Under this conception, a fledgling regional organization like APEC could become the vanguard of liberalization in a post-Uruguay Round world (Bergsten, 1994).

Japanese support for "open regionalism," however, does not mean that Tokyo will necessarily stay in step with Washington in promoting trade and investment liberalization agreements. In fact, the Japanese are relatively reluctant to push for formal rules. They prefer what some have called "organic economic integration guided by market mechanisms" (Kobayashi, Nakamura, Ito, and Watanabe, 1994, pp. 28–30). This vague concept refers to an integration that emerges as a result of "market liberalization, direct investment, and official development" and that respects the region's diversity in economic standards, ethnic groups, religions, and political systems. In other words, a regional economic order is not to be constructed according to prior international rules and regulations, but rather an order is to emanate organically or naturally from increasing intraregional economic interaction, cross-investments, and personal and cultural exchanges.

This attitude toward regionalism will place Japan right in the middle of the tension between the Anglo-American states (especially the United States), which favor formal negotiations of common rules of economic behavior, and many of the East Asian states, which are apprehensive of America's ideological commitment to trade liberalization and zealous interference in domestic policies and politics. Japan's first preference is to play the role of bridging the gap between the United States and East Asia. On the one hand, Japan will want to support the U.S. liberalization agenda in East Asia in order to defuse bilateral economic tensions and to revitalize the U.S.-Japan security alliance. On the other hand, it will seek to develop an "Asian identity" and articulate Asian concerns to the United States. In short, Japan will want to have it both ways, and it will seek to avoid ever having to make a choice.

Whether or not Japan will have to make such a choice will depend upon how tolerant the United States will be about the current state of affairs—a situation in which East Asian penetration into the U.S. market far exceeds American penetration into East Asian markets. An intolerant America could move in one of two directions. It could adopt protectionist measures against East Asian imports either in a unilateral manner or in the context of NAFTA. Or it could aggressively promote regional economic liberalization in coalition with other Anglo-American states. Responding to these two alternatives will certainly fracture the current Japanese political consensus for an open regionalism that bridges America and East Asia. How Japan chooses to respond will depend upon how much its foreign economic interests (as measured in terms of trade, investments, and technology flows) will have shifted from North America to East Asia and how many East Asian allies it could mobilize to resist or counter the United States. The more that Japan's center of economic gravity has shifted to East Asia and the more that it is able to win regional allies, the more likely that Japan will refuse to accommodate American pressures.

In the meantime, the Japanese are likely to pursue a hedging strategy. Tokyo's approach to the East Asian Economic Caucus (EAEC) reflects such an approach. In one sense, the Japanese see the EAEC as a benign and natural expression of an "Asian identity" and a positive mechanism to counter (or deter) discriminatory or exclusionary measures coming from NAFTA. At the same time, however, Tokyo policymakers are wary that formalization of EAEC even within the APEC framework could needlessly aggravate relations with the United States. Therefore, they have resisted ASEAN proposals to make the EAEC into a voting bloc within APEC. The strongest proponents of caution regarding the EAEC are the MOFA officials responsible for North American policy. But their grip on this issue is tenuous. There is growing support within political and business circles for a closer political relationship with East Asian countries as a hedge against a worsening of relations with the United States.

Chapter Six

CONCLUSIONS

The current process of domestic change holds the promise of producing a Japan that would be more supportive of U.S. interests. In the political-military realm, political realignment and the emergence of a more consensual defense policymaking process could make Japan into a more active security partner. Either of the two alternatives of great power internationalism or civilian internationalism would lessen America's burden for maintaining international security—albeit in different ways. Both paths would be healthy outlets for Japanese nationalism. In the economic realm, policy choices and market forces could make Japan into a more open economy that provides greater access to foreign firms and gives greater weight to consumer interests relative to those of producers. In terms of regional policy, Japan could become a nation more willing to take diplomatic risks to support America's interests and values in East Asia as well as to develop multilateral institutions for maintaining regional stability.

Despite the promise of these positive outcomes, developments that would be adverse to U.S. interests are also possible. First, the political realignment process now under way could lead to a prolonged period of political instability and weak governments. Such a situation would make it difficult, if not impossible, for Japan to take decisive and timely action to deal with international security crises (in both the Asia-Pacific region and elsewhere) in cooperation with the United States. A Japanese government in disarray would also shy away from making the hard choices needed to establish a more stable equilibrium in U.S.-Japan economic relations, much less to strengthen the liberal international economic order. Under such circumstances, bureaucratic agencies would reemerge as the drivers of economic policy and undermine efforts at deregulation. A critical indicator of such a scenario would come soon after the first general election under the new electoral system. Although the new system is designed to encourage aggregation of political forces into two large political parties in a competitive party system, a failure to do so either before or after the election would be a clear harbinger of prolonged instability and weak governments.

Second, domestic change could lead to political repolarization and ultimately the ascendancy of great power nationalism, which would involve a security strategy independent from or less cooperative with the United States. A combination of political and economic factors could produce such an outcome. In an era of international uncertainty and change, prolonged political instability could cause Japanese citizens to feel that their nation is being buffeted by hostile external forces. If Japan is unable to make the structural adjustments necessary to revitalize the economy while keeping the social pain of such adjustments to a minimum, then domestic support for a more assertive and independent foreign policy backed by a stronger military is likely to increase. At the same time, the influx of foreign workers and the social problems associated with it could trigger a nationalistic backlash similar to that now found in Western Europe. These interrelated developments would have an effect beyond weakening the U.S.-Japan security relationship. They would also alarm Japan's Asian neighbors and exacerbate the distrust that persists in the region. Ultimately, uncontrolled geopolitical rivalry precipitated by a militarily autonomous Japan would dramatically increase U.S. risks and costs for maintaining stability in Pacific Asia.

The critical indicators of this adverse scenario involve the following:

- Failure to aggregate the various domestic political forces into a two-party system or to develop stable coalition governments under a moderate multiparty system (no more than four major parties).

- Emergence of a stridently nationalistic political party that is able to win at least 10 percent of the votes.

- Prolonged (e.g., over a five-year period) low (less than 2 percent) or negative annual economic growth rates.

- Officially reported unemployment rates exceeding 5 percent.

- Increase in the influx of foreign workers and a sharp rise in social problems associated with these workers.

- Increasing number of mainstream (and heretofore pro-American) intellectuals who are critical of U.S. foreign economic and security policies.

- Public opinion surveys indicating greater negative attitudes toward the United States (e.g., less than 55 percent expressing an affinity toward the United States and/or more than 25 percent expressing hostility toward the United States) and greater support for an autonomous security strategy based upon a stronger military (over 20 percent of the respondents).

Third, a failure by Japan to shift away from neomercantilist economic policies and business practices by either choice or indecision could have adverse consequences for the United States. Such a Japan is likely to *openly* resist American pressures on a variety of trade and investment issues, which could in turn provoke unilateral measures from the United States. Thus far, Tokyo has responded to American unilateralism on the economic front in a relatively accommodative manner. But as the Japanese economy becomes further integrated with East Asia and less dependent upon U.S. markets, Tokyo may be increasingly tempted to rebuff Washington's unilateral actions and even to retaliate in kind. A spiraling trade war will certainly lead to a political estrangement between these two allies and may even ultimately provoke a rupture in the bilateral security relationship.

Quite apart from its effect on the U.S.-Japan relationship, Japanese neomercantilism, by persisting, would also intensify the economic competition among East Asian countries, especially if the U.S. market became less receptive to Asian imports. Of course, intra-Asian economic competition in itself is not necessarily bad. Indeed such competition could yield positive economic gains for all countries in the region and sustain the region's economic dynamism. But the problem with neomercantilism is that it leads to the "export" of the social costs of domestic economic adjustment and highlights *relative*, as opposed to absolute, economic gains. Thus, the danger is that other East Asian countries will fear either Japanese economic exploitation or economic domination. This pattern of transnational economic linkages would exacerbate, rather than mitigate, the historical geopolitical tensions that still exist in the region.

Early indicators of this adverse outcome would include the following:

- Emergence of interparty and government consensus to resist more openly U.S. pressures for economic liberalization backed by a reinvigorated protectionist coalition of farmers, small businesses, and workers.

- Persistence or increase of Japan's high overall trade and current account surpluses (over $100 billion per year for both statistics), of its high bilateral trade surplus with the United States (over $50 billion per year), and of its high trade surplus with East Asian economies as a whole (over $40 billion per year).

- Increasing number of mainstream intellectuals who are critical of U.S. foreign economic policies and who stress the strengths of Japan's model of capitalism and the weaknesses of the Anglo-American liberal model.

- Increasing public support for a non-accommodative stance toward U.S. pressures for more open markets as reflected in opinion surveys (over 50 percent of respondents).

A fourth adverse outcome of domestic change would be a Japanese foreign policy that seeks to develop a regional security and/or economic system that decreases U.S. political/military and economic leverage and presence in the region. Currently such a scenario seems farfetched because Japan and other East Asian countries see U.S. markets as critical to their economic success and U.S. military presence in the region as necessary to preserve a stable balance of power. But as East Asian markets increase in importance relative to the U.S. market for Japanese businesses, policy elites may be tempted to cultivate economic relationships with other East Asian countries that place U.S. firms at a disadvantage. Moreover, Japanese leaders may become more receptive to calls for an East Asian economic grouping that excludes the Anglo-American states in the Asia-Pacific region. Even short of that, Tokyo could articulate more forcefully in APEC meetings the perspective of East Asian countries in resisting the liberalizing impulses of Anglo-American members. In terms of security affairs, current efforts at cultivating multilateral security dialogues are designed to complement, not replace, the Japanese and other East Asian security linkages with the United States. But the more confident Japan becomes about its ability to manage relations with China, Korea, and the major states of Southeast Asia on its own, the more it will be tempted to devalue its security relationship with the United States. An overly hostile U.S. policy toward these East Asia actors (e.g., in terms of human rights and democratization) would certainly reinforce this tendency.

Indicators of this fourth adverse scenario include the following:

- Emergence of major political parties that articulate a pan-Asian foreign policy as a viable alternative to a pro-American, pro-Western foreign policy.

- Increase in the importance of the East Asian region relative to North America for trade and investments (for example, if Japan's trade with and investments in East Asia were to exceed its trade with and investments in North America by over 50 percent).

- Increase in mainstream intellectuals who emphasize Japan's identity with East Asia as opposed to that with the West and the need to develop a regional economic and/or security system in which the role of the United States is less prominent.

- Increasing public affinity toward major East Asian countries, especially China, relative to a decreasing affinity toward the United States.

BIBLIOGRAPHY

Aoki, Masahiko, "Toward an Economic Model of the Japanese Firm," *Journal of Economic Literature*, Vol. 28, 1990, pp. 1–27.

Asahi Shimbun Seijibu, *Renritsu seiken mawari butai*, Tokyo: Asahi Shimbunsha, 1994.

Bauer, John, "Demographic Change and Asian Labor Markets in the 1990s," *Population and Development Review*, Vol. 16, No. 4, 1990, pp. 615–645.

Bergsten, C. Fred, "APEC and World Trade: A Force for Worldwide Liberalization," *Foreign Affairs*, Vol. 73, No. 3, May/June 1994, pp. 20–26.

Bernard, Mitchell, and John Ravenhill, "Beyond Product Cycles and Flying Geese: Regionalization, Hierarchy, and the Industrialization of East Asia," *World Politics*, Vol. 47, January 1995, pp. 171–209.

Bo'ei Cho, ed., *Bo'ei Hakusho*, Tokyo: Okurasho Insatsu Kyoku, 1993.

Calder, Kent E., *Crisis and Compensation: Public Policy and Political Stability in Japan, 1949–1986*, Princeton: Princeton University Press, 1988.

Calder, Kent E. , *Strategic Capitalism: Private Business and Public Purpose in Japanese Industrial Finance*, Princeton: Princeton University Press, 1993.

Chuma, Hiroyuki, *Nihon gata 'Koyo chosei,'* Tokyo: Shueisha, 1994.

Clark, Robert, and Naohiro Ogawa, "Employment Tenure and Earning Profiles in Japan and the United States: Comment, *American Economic Review*, Vol. 82, No. 1, 1992, pp. 336–345.

Defense Agency officials, interviews, Tokyo, October 4, and December 20, 1993.

Defense Issues Discussion Group (DIDG), *Nihon no anzen hosho to bo'ei ryuoku no arikata: 21 seiki e mukete no tenbo* presented to Prime Minister Murayama on August 12, 1994.

Department of Defense, Office of International Security Affairs, *United States Security Strategy for the East Asia–Pacific Region*, Washington, D.C.: Department of Defense, February 1995.

Dobson, Wendy, *Japan in East Asia: Trading and Investment Strategies*, Singapore: Institute of Southeast Studies, 1993.

Ebata, Kensuke, *Ebata Kensuke no senso senryaku ron I: Chugoku ga kubo o motsu hi*, Tokyo: Tokuma Shoten, 1994.

Emmott, Bill, *The Sun Also Sets: The Limits of Japan's Economic Power*, New York: Times Books, Random House, 1989.

Farnsworth, Clyde H., "U.S. Concern over Japan's Surplus," *The New York Times*, June 14, 1990, p. D2.

Frankel, Jeffrey A., "Is Japan Creating a Yen Bloc in East Asia and the Pacific," in Jeffrey A. Frankel and Miles Kahler, eds., *Regionalism and Rivalry: Japan and the United States in Pacific Asia*, Chicago: The University of Chicago Press, 1993, pp. 53–85.

Funabashi, Yoichi, *Nihon no taigai koso: Reisen go no bijon o kaku*, Tokyo: Iwanami Shoten, 1993.

Garon, Sheldon, and Mike Mochizuki, "Negotiating Social Contracts," in Andrew Gordon, ed., *Postwar Japan as History*, Berkeley: University of California Press, 1993, pp. 145–166.

Gerlach, Michael L., *Alliance Capitalism: The Social Organization of Japanese Business*, Berkeley: University of California Press, 1992.

Goto, Juichi, *Ikeda Daisaku vs Ozawa Ichiro*, Tokyo: Ginga Shuppan, 1994.

Graham, Edward M., and Naoko T. Anzai, "The Myth of a De Facto Asian Economic Bloc: Japan's Foreign Direct Investment in East Asia," *Columbia Journal of World Business*, Vol. 29, No. 3, Fall 1994, pp. 6–20.

Ground Self-Defense Force, retired Japanese general, personal interview, Tokyo, October 5, 1993.

Gyoten, Toyoo, *Nihon keizai no shiza*, Tokyo: Kobunsha, 1993.

Hiwatari, Nobuhiro, *Sengo Nihon shijo to seiji*, Tokyo: Tokyo Daigaku Shuppankai, 1991.

Ienaga, Saburo, *The Pacific War: World War II and the Japanese, 1931–1945*, New York: Pantheon Books, 1978.

Ishihara, Shintaro, "Kaku no kasa de on o uru na," in Ishihara Shintaro, Watanabe Shoichi, Ogawa Kazuhisa, Sore demo, eds., *"No" to ieru Nippon*, Tokyo: Kobunsha, 1990, pp. 55–56.

Ishihara, Shintaro, and Morita Akio, *"No" to ieru Nippon*, Tokyo: Kobunsha, 1989.

Ishihara, Shintaro, and Mohamad Mahathir, *"No" to ieru Ajia*, Tokyo: Kobunsha, 1994.

Itagaki, Hidenori, *Heisei doran: Ozawa Ichiro no yabo*, Tokyo: DHC, 1993.

Itagaki, Hidenori, *Takemura Masayoshi no makyaberizumu*, Tokyo: DHC, 1994.

Japan Economic Institute, *JEI Report: Statistical Profile—Japan's Economy and International Transactions of Japan and the United States*, Washington, D.C.: Japan Economic Institute, October 13, 1989, and September 16, 1994.

Johnson, Chalmers, *MITI and the Japanese Miracle: The Growth of Industrial Policy, 1925–1975*, Stanford: Stanford University Press, 1982.

Kajita, Takamichi, *Gaikokujin rodosha to Nihon*, Tokyo: NHK Bukkusu, 1994.

Kamo, Takehiko, *Sekai seiji o doo miru ka,* Tokyo: Iwanami Shoten, 1993.

Kato, Hiroshi, *Aete tou Nihon no han'ei,* Tokyo: Zeimu keiri kyokai, 1990.

Keizai Doyu Kai (Japan Association of Corporate Executives), "Restructuring the Japanese Economy: From Concept to Implementation," November 1994.

Keizai Kikakucho, *Bukka Report,* Tokyo: Okurasho Insatsu Kyoku, 1994.

Keizai Kikakucho, *Kokumin Keizai Keisan Nempo,* Tokyo: Okura-sho Insatsu Kyoku, published annually.

Kisei Kanwa Kenkyukai, ed., *Kisei kanwa de Nihon ga kawaru,* Tokyo: *The Japan Times,* 1994.

Kobayashi, Minoru, Jin Nakamura, Motoshige Ito, and Kazuo Watanabe, *The Future of Regionalism and Japan,* Tokyo: The Japan Forum on International Relations, Inc., June 1994.

Kosai, Yutaka, and Uchida Shigeo, *Nihon keizai fuea-pure sengen,* Tokyo: Nihon Keizai Shimbunsha, 1993.

LDP National Diet member in the Mitsuzuka faction, interview, December 1993.

Lincoln, Edward J., *Japan's New Global Role,* Washington, D.C.: The Brookings Institution, 1993.

Masamura, Kimihiro, *Seijuku shakai e no sentaku,* Tokyo: Nihon Hoso Shuppan Kyokai, 1994.

Mason, Mark, "Foreign Direct Investment in East Asia: Trends and Critical U.S. Policy Issues," *Asia Project Working Paper,* New York: Council on Foreign Relations, November 1994.

Masuzoe, Yoichi, *Seikai dai sai-hen,* Tokyo: Sandoke Shuppankyoku, 1994.

McNeil, Frank, *Democracy in Japan: The Emerging Global Concern,* New York: Crown Publishers, 1994.

McNeil, Frank, *Japanese Politics: Decay or Reform?* Washington, D.C.: The Carnegie Endowment for International Peace, 1993.

Moriguchi, Shigeru, "Current and Future Investment Outlook in Asia," *Journal of Japanese Trade and Industry,* Vol. 14, No. 2, March/April 1995, pp. 8–10.

Morita, Akira, "Shin jiyu keizai e no teigen," *Bungei Shunju,* February 1993, pp. 94–109.

Morita, Akira, "Toward a New World Economic Order," *The Atlantic Monthly,* June 1993, pp. 88–98.

Murakami, Yasusuke, "The Japanese Model of Political Economy," in Kozo Yamamura and Yasukichi Yasuba, eds., *The Political Economy of Japan: Vol. 1, The Domestic Transformation,* Stanford: Stanford University Press, 1987.

Nagai, Yonosuke, "Moritoriamu kokka no bo'ei ron," *Chuo Koron,* January 1981.

Nakasone, Yasuhiro, Sato Seizaburo, Murakami Yasusuke, and Nishibe Susumu, *Kyodo kenkyu: "Resisen igo,"* Tokyo: Bungei Shunju, 1992.

Nakatani, Iwao, "Heisei dai fukyo e no shohoosen," *This Is Yomiuri,* November 1993, pp. 43–53.

NHK Television, "Nichi-yo toron," May 22, 1994.

NHK Yoron Chosabu, ed., *Gendai Nihonjin no ishiki kozo,* 3rd edition, Tokyo: NHK Bukkusu, 1991.

Nihon Keizai Shimbunsha, ed., *Kanryo: kishimu kyodai kenryoku,* Tokyo: Nihon Keizai Shimbunsha, 1994.

Noguchi, Yukio, *Nihon keizai: kaikaku no kozu,* Tokyo: Toyo Keizai Shinposha, 1993.

Noland, Marcus, "Implication of Asian Economic Growth," *Asia Project Working Paper,* New York: Council on Foreign Relations, November 1994.

Ogura, Kazuo, "A Call for a New Concept of Asia," *Japan Echo,* Vol. 20, No. 3, Autumn 1993, p. 44. Originally published in Japanese as "'Ajia no fukken' no tame ni," *Chuo Koron,* July 1993, pp. 60–73.

Oka, Takashi, *Prying Open the Door: Foreign Workers in Japan,* Washington, D.C.: Carnegie Endowment for International Peace, 1994, p. 62.

Okazaki, Hisahiko, *Kokusai josei no mikata,* Tokyo: Shinchosha, 1994.

Okazaki, Hisahiko, "Southeast Asia in Japan's National Strategy," *Japan Echo,* Vol. 20 (Special Issue), 1993, pp. 60–63. Originally published in Japanese as "'Ajia chotaiken' e no shinsenryaku," *This Is Yomiuri,* August 1992, pp. 42–90.

Okazaki, Hisahiko, and Hajime Izumi, "Nihon ga sansen suru tejun," *Voice,* June 1994, pp. 102 and 105.

Okimoto, Daniel I., *Between MITI and the Market: Japanese Industrial Policy for High Technology,* Stanford: Stanford University Press, 1989.

Pollack, Andrew, "Japan's Jobless Rate at Highest Level Ever," *The New York Times,* May 31, 1995.

Pyle, Kenneth B., *The Japanese Question: Power and Purpose in a New Era,* Washington, D.C.: The AEI Press, 1992.

Reading, Brian, *Japan: The Coming Collapse,* New York: Harper Business, 1992.

Rinji Gyosei Kaikaku Suishin Shingikai Jimushitsu, *Kisei kanwa no suishin,* Tokyo: Gyosei, 1989.

Ryuzaki, Takashi, *Ozawa Ichiro no gyakushu,* Tokyo: Sankei Shuppankyoku, 1993.

Saito, Naoki, "The Passing of the PKO Cooperation Law: Japan's Struggle to Define Its International Contribution," *IIGP Policy Paper 102E,* Tokyo: International Institute for Global Peace, November 1992.

Sakakibara, Eisuke, *Bummei toshite no Nihon-gata shihonshugi*, Tokyo: Toyo Keizai Shimposha, 1993.

Sato, Seizaburo, "Seiji kaikaku: yattsu no gobyu," *Chuo Koron*, October 1993, pp. 106–117.

Sato, Yoshio, *Ozawa Ichiro no anyaku o sasaeru Rengo*, Tokyo: Shakai Shihyo Sha, 1993.

Sawa, Takamitsu, *Heisei fukyo no seiji keizai gaku*, Tokyo: Chuo Koronsha, 1994.

Schlesinger, Jacob M., "Tokyo, Keeping Options Open, Hesitates to Sign Indefinite Nuclear Arms Treaty," *Wall Street Journal*, July 12, 1993.

Suzuki, Yoshio, "Prospects for the Japanese Economy," unpublished paper, April 1995.

Suzuki, Yoshio, "Short Comments on Krugman's Paper 'The Myth of Asia's Miracle,'" *Sisa Journal*, February 2–9, 1995.

Tajima, Yoshihiro, *Kisei kanwa*, Tokyo: NHK bukkusu, 1994.

Takemura, Masayoshi, *Chisaku tomo kirari to hikaru kuni: Nihon*, Tokyo: Kobunsha, 1994.

Tanaka, Shusei, *Sakigake to seiken kotai*, Tokyo: Toyo Keizai Shinposha, 1994.

Urata, Shujiro, "Changing Patterns of Direct Investment and the Implications for Trade and Development," in C. Fred Bergsten and Marcus Noland, eds., *Pacific Dynamism and the International Economic System*, Washington, D.C.: Institute for International Economics, 1993, pp. 273–297.

Watanabe, Kensuke, *Ano hito: hitotsu no Ozawa Ichiro ron*, Tokyo: Asuka Shinsha, 1992.

Watanabe, Michio, Kakizawa Koji, and Ibuki Bummei, *Shin hoshu kakumei*, Tokyo: Nesuco, 1994.

Watanuki, Joji, "Nihonjin no kokusai shakai kan ni tsuite no jissho-teki kenkyu—1972 nen to 1992 nen," *Institute of International*

Relations Research Papers C-8, Tokyo: Jochi Daigaku Kokusai Kankei Kenkyujo, December 1993.

Yamamoto, Tsuyoshi, "Kita Chosen o kataru zentei to wa," *Sekai*, October 1993, pp. 262–263.

Yamashita, Masamitsu, Takai Susumu, and Iwata Shuichiro, *TMD: Sen-iki dando misairu bo'ei*, Tokyo: TBS Buritanika, 1994.

Yashiro, Naohiro, "Japan's Economy in the Year 2020—The Complementary Relationship Between the Aging of the Population and Internationalization of the Economy," *JCER Report*, Vol. 7, No. 3, March 1995, pp. 3–6.

Yayama, Taro, *Kanryo bokoku ron*, Tokyo: Shinchosha, 1993.

The Yomiuri Constitution Study Council, *The First Proposal*, December 9, 1992.

Yomiuri Shimbunsha, ed., *Kempo: 21 seiki ni mukete*, Tokyo: Yomiuri Shimbunsha, 1994.

Yoron Chosa, Tokyo: Okurasho Insatsukyoku, April 1993 and April 1994.

"Zeisei kaikaku de seiji kyusen o," *This Is Yomiuri*, November 1993, p. 27.